GWG0733962

English Teaching Perspectives

Donn Byrne

Longman

Longman Group Limited,
Longman House, Burnt Mill, Harlow,
Essex CM20 2JE, England
and Associated Companies throughout the world

© Longman Group Ltd. 1980

First published 1980
Fourth impression 1985

ISBN 0 582 74604 3

Produced by Longman Singapore Publishers Pte Ltd.
Printed in Singapore.

Preface

Over ten years have passed since the publication of *English Teaching Extracts* and, although teachers and teacher trainers continue to find this material useful, it now has two main defects. First, inevitably, many of the viewpoints expressed in the extracts have become dated. This is no cause for regret, since it would be a sad reflection on 'the state of the art' if our knowledge had not progressed and our opinions had not accordingly changed (not that changes of opinion necessarily reflect progress in knowledge!). Secondly, and again perhaps inevitably, certain aspects of methodology are not dealt with at all in *English Teaching Extracts* or are only touched on in passing. For a book aimed in particular at the beginning teacher these two defects cannot be lightly dismissed. For this reason, although many of the texts in *English Teaching Extracts* are still relevant to teacher training, it seemed better to embark on a completely new selection rather than to attempt a revision.

The task of identifying and selecting suitable *short* extracts has proved to be an arduous one, mainly because of the sheer amount of material on language teaching now available. Likewise, putting the texts in an acceptable order and organising them into sections has not been easy. One fundamental issue that had to be resolved was whether to begin with a consideration of certain theoretical issues concerning language, which might prove difficult for teachers with little or no familiarity with applied linguistics, or with more 'practical' matters directly related to the classroom. In the end, I decided to follow what seemed to be the logical progression: from a discussion of language through to the teaching of language. It rests with the user of this book to decide for himself whether this is the order which best suits his needs.

My sources for *English Teaching Perspectives* have been books and articles, both British and American, which have been published for the most part over the last ten years. From these there emerges, I hope, a clear emphasis on the need to teach language as a means of communication. At the same time, I have not tried to exclude, in the hope of presenting a more uniform viewpoint, certain topics which, although not directly related to a communicative approach to language teaching, need to be discussed as part of the broader context of classroom teaching. It might be felt, for example, that there is no need to discuss a topic such as choral work (or 'collective speaking' as it is called in 5.1). However, there are teachers working with classes of upwards of forty pupils who need to understand the advantages and disadvantages of this procedure and for whom it is important to evaluate its effectiveness alongside alternative procedures such as pair work and group work. Even teachers in privileged teaching situations would do well to consider its possible relevance for certain purposes.

Within the modest limits of the material and the purposes for which it is intended (see the *Introduction*), I hope I have managed to assemble a collection of texts which will prove as useful and workable as *English Teaching Extracts*. At the same time, even before the book goes into circulation, I am deeply conscious of its many defects and omissions.

Contents

Introduction

English Teaching Perspectives is intended in particular for use with the following:

(a) teachers who are native speakers of English preparing for examinations such as the RSA;

(b) teachers who are not native speakers of English attending pre-service or in-service training courses or preparing for the RSA examination overseas;

(c) teachers who meet in groups on a voluntary basis to discuss teaching problems.

For all these categories *English Teaching Perspectives* is designed, as the title suggests, to provide an overview of key aspects of language teaching methodology. For (b) this collection of texts is also intended to meet a special need – to familiarise teachers with the language needed to talk and read about language teaching. Like *English Teaching Extracts,* this book can be used to prepare trainee teachers for extensive reading on methodology. The approach is one of exposure – but it is gentle exposure, through relatively short texts, since complete books and articles can be daunting in the early stages of training. This aim accomplished, teachers must be encouraged to read on a wide scale. This collection is a preparation for but not an alternative to such wider reading.

As with *English Teaching Extracts*, in preparing this book I have tried to keep in mind the teacher-training situation, both on short courses and on ones of longer duration, where certain aspects of methodology may be profitably discussed in small groups either as a follow-up to a formal talk or as an alternative to it. The text should be carefully studied before the tutorial period, together with the questions which follow each text. These may be selected according to the needs of the class. In this way each text will provide a positive framework for discussion, which the tutor in charge of the group will be able to guide and participate in without monopolising all the talking time.

The questions and discussion points following each text may also be used for written assignments if these form part of the course. Some of these, particularly the ones concerned with the examination and evaluation of teaching materials with which the trainees are familiar, can also be used as the basis for project work.

For the teachers' groups referred to in (c) above, a similar approach may be followed. It is hoped that the material in this book will provide a series of focal points for preparation before a group meeting and for discussion and exchange of ideas during it.

In any of the teacher-training situations in which this book is used, some follow-up work is likely to be needed and for this purpose a bibliography has been provided for each extract. Frequent reference is made to certain standard works on English language teaching, with chapter or page references, and to journals or collections of articles commonly available.

With regard to the organisation of the material in this book, the section headings are intended to provide a guide to the *focus* of each section. Section 1 – *Aspects of Language and Language Learning* – provides a certain amount of 'background' information about language, while Section 2 deals with issues which, for want of a better word, are theoretical rather than practical. With Section 3 we come on to matters more directly concerned with what goes on in the classroom. Sections 4 and 5 complement each other: it seemed useful to have some discussion of the skills of listening, speaking, reading and writing apart from a consideration of certain techniques and procedures, but the dividing line between these two sections is less distinct than in other parts of the book. Teacher trainers would be well advised to familiarise themselves with the total range of material in these two sections to decide how best the texts may be related to suit the particular needs of their trainees.

PROLOGUE

Methodology should be based on what we know about language (what it is and how it operates – still a matter of controversy); what we know about human beings (how they learn and how they learn language and whether these are different processes or merely different manifestations of the same process – another question which is still under investigation); and what we know about people in interaction (a prolific area of psychological study). It is inevitable, then, that methodological recommendations will change as our knowledge of these three factors evolves, with earlier postulates being rejected and new premises accepted. Teachers should keep in touch with findings in these areas and share the excitement of a developing and progressing discipline.

W Rivers
Speaking in Many Tongues
(Newbury House 1972) p 5

Section 1
Aspects of Language and Language Learning

1.1 What is Language?

Language is a very complex thing, and it cannot yet be fully accounted for by anyone within one wholly consistent and comprehensive theory. Certainly linguists have found it so. For this reason, when asked the question *What is language?*, the linguist is
5 likely to reply by asking another question *Why do you want to know?* If we teach language, the way we approach our task will be influenced, or even determined, by what we believe language to be, by the particular informal theory or theories we have about it which seem to be relevant to the particular problem we are faced with.
10 There is generally a close connection between the way we talk about something and the way we regard it. The language we use about it betrays our views on what it is. If we want to know what someone believes language is, we must listen to the language he uses to talk about it. If we do this we soon notice that people seem to hold
15 at one and the same time incompatible views about its nature. For example, we regularly hear people talking about 'using language': *He used some awful language*; *He used a word I didn't understand*; *What use is French?* This suggests that language is an object like a tool, which we can pick up, use for some purpose and put down
20 again. People sometimes even actually call language a tool. We also talk about people 'possessing' a language. Shakespeare was reported by Jonson as *having* 'small Latin and less Greek'. Children are said to 'acquire' language. Apparently we sometimes 'lose' it: *I can't find the right word.* Now, if language was solely regarded as behaviour of
25 a particular sort this would be a very strange way of talking about it. Can we talk about 'walking' in the same way? Can we say that we 'use' walking to get somewhere, or 'acquire', 'possess' or 'lose' walking?
Linguists, especially, often talk about how language 'works', as if
30 it were an object like an alarm clock, whose functioning could be understood from a study of its internal structure of springs and cogwheels. It is significant that while a study of the internal structure of a clock will tell you *how* it works, it won't tell you what clocks are *for*. This notion of internal structure evidently lies behind such
35 statements as: *This sentence has a complex structure* or, in teaching, the phrase: *Learning a new construction.* Although we typically think

13

of mechanisms as being lifeless objects, we frequently refer to language as if it were a living organism. We speak about the 'birth' of a language, of its 'growth', 'development' and 'decline'. Languages
40 have periods of 'blossoming' and 'flowering' (always in the past); they are 'related' to each other in 'families', or 'descended' from each other. They are 'living' or 'dead'. They also have physical and moral qualities; they are 'beautiful', 'ugly', 'vulgar', 'debased' or 'decadent'.

45 I am not seriously suggesting that people actually believe that language is a concrete object which can be physically handled like a tool. These ways of talking about language are metaphorical. But it is interesting that we have to resort to metaphor to talk about language at all. The metaphors all have this in common, though:
50 they all treat language as an *object*. They 'reify' language.

We also find people talking about language as an 'event'. A conversation 'takes place', words 'crop up' in a discussion. We even speak about someone's speech as 'the event of the evening'.

Language is something we 'know'. We ask someone if he 'knows'
55 French or German, or if he 'knows' some word or other. It is also something we 'do'. We write, read, speak well or badly. In this case we are treating it as skilled behaviour which we have to learn, and which improves through practice.

Our language about language reveals a variety of different ways of
60 regarding it which, even if we admit that they are often meta- phorical, nevertheless imply a certain logical inconsistency. The question is not so much which of these views is 'right'; they are all in their way valid, but none of them is complete or comprehensive. We just have to admit that language is such a complex phenomenon that
65 no one viewpoint can see it as a whole. The question we really need to ask is not which view is 'right', but which view is useful, which view is relevant to language teaching. Can we say that any of the approaches to language as knowledge, as behaviour, as skill, as habit, as an event or an object can safely be disregarded by the language
70 teacher?

S Pit Corder
Introducing Applied Linguistics (Penguin Education 1973) pp 19–21

1 *'If we want to know what someone believes language is, we must listen to the language he uses to talk about it'* (lines 12–14).

a What ways of looking at language are mentioned by the author?

b   The author mentions various ways in which English speakers talk about language. Do speakers of other languages use the same or similar expressions when talking about language?
c   What conclusions does the author draw from our 'language about language'?

2 What is *your* answer to the question which the author asks at the end of the passage? Do you think that any of the approaches to language which he mentions is especially important for the language teacher?

FOR FURTHER REFERENCE
1   J Wallwork *Language and Linguistics* (Heinemann Educational 1969) Chapter 1.
2   D Bolinger *Aspects of Language* (Harcourt Brace 1968) Chapter 2.
3   A E Darbyshire *A Description of English* (Arnold 1969) Chapter 1.
4   M Finocchiaro *English as a Second Language* (Regents 1974) pp 1–13.

1.2 Language as Communication

Language is a means of communication. Although not the only form of communication among human beings, it is certainly the most important. Our entire elaborate social structure is mediated through language, and it is inconceivable that we could have constructed so
5 complex a social interaction if we had not had spoken and, latterly written language at our disposal. Language is central to human experience and if we are to understand the process by which men communicate with one another, we must look closely at the human capacity for language and at the particular qualities of language
10 which enable it to play so powerful a role within us and between us.

We might well begin by considering just how successfully we do communicate through language. We find in fact that we have a remarkable versatility. We never know what we are going to need to communicate and yet when the time comes, as mature speakers of
15 the language, provided the necessary knowledge and experience itself is not lacking, we have no difficulty in expressing whatever it may be we have the need to express. Whether we are involved in day-to-day interaction with members of our family, in complex ex-planations of unforeseen events, in emotional reactions to un-
20 expected happenings, in the familiar or unfamiliar alike, we can quite unconsciously apply our knowledge of language to meeting the demands of what we need to say or write. Nor is this in some way a feat of memory. We do not know how to express ourselves because we have often had to do so in the same or similar ways in the past. It
25 is very rare that what we wish to express now is exactly the same as something we have wanted to say previously. There is usually some difference of emphasis, of conviction or of situation at the very least. In other words, the demands that we want to place on language are virtually limitless.
30   It is perhaps the most important characteristic of language that it is formed in a way that enables us to meet these demands. Just as life itself places us in situations which are never twice quite the same, so language enables us continually to express novel propositions. Our faculty of language is a faculty of linguistic creativity. Most of the
35 sentences we utter have never been constructed by us previously and many, indeed, have never been constructed by anyone else either.

There is literally no limit to the number of sentences we can create in English.

How is language organised to meet the demands that the individual's desire to communicate will place upon it? As well as possessing a set of grammatical rules through which linguistic creativity is achieved, language contains a system of symbols by means of which we can refer to entities in the physical world and can express more abstract concepts. These symbols constitute the vocabulary or lexicon of the language and they are listed in a dictionary. The way in which the grammatical system is applied in the actual process of communication depends on features of the individuals involved, the setting in which the communication takes place and the purpose of the users. These factors can consistently influence the speaker's choice of linguistic forms. Finally, there are rules governing the way in which language is expressed physically, either as sound or as visible shapes on paper. Except for intonation, the phonic or graphic substance of language contributes only indirectly to meaning. The native speaker's linguistic competence is made up of a knowledge of all these aspects of language.

D Wilkins
Second Language Learning and Teaching (Arnold 1974) pp 1–4
abridged

1 The author says that language is the most important means of communication among human beings.
 a How does he justify this statement?
 b Give examples of other forms of communication.

2 *'Language . . . is formed in a way that enables us to meet these demands* (lines 30–31).
 a What are the demands which the author is referring to?
 b Why does he say that these demands are not met through 'a feat of memory'?
 c How is language organised to meet these demands?

3 What is meant by the faculty of 'linguistic creativity'?

4 Give your opinion of the relevance of the concept of 'linguistic creativity' for second language learning.

FOR FURTHER REFERENCE

1 D Crystal *Linguistics* (Penguin 1971) pp 14–19.

2 G Broughton et al. *Teaching English as a Second Language* (Routledge and Kegan Paul 1978) Chapter 3.

3 J W Oller in P Pimsleur and T Quinn (Eds) *The Psychology of Second Language Learning* (CUP 1971) *Language Communication and Second Language Learning.*

1.3 Language and Culture

Language and culture are inexorably intertwined. Language is at once an outcome or a result of the culture as a whole and also a vehicle by which the other facets of the culture are shaped and communicated. The language we learn as a child gives us not only a
5 system for communication, but, more important, it dictates the type and form of the communications we make. The universe is ordered in accordance with the way we name it. An Eskimo would think us extremely vague if we told him it was snowing. His language provides him with a universe that encompasses dozens of types of
10 'snowing'. In the same way we would consider the Eskimo vague if he made an appointment with us for 'some time later'. To the North American, time is a real commodity. He can waste time, spend time, charge for time, kill time, pass time, sell time, and be on time or in time. Our language reflects and reinforces our cultural patterns and
15 value system.
  The sounds and patterns that we learn as our first language cause what have been described as linguistic blind spots. While learning our native language we are trained not only to produce certain sounds, which are rewarded, but we are also rewarded not to
20 produce other sounds. We are trained to ignore and ultimately not to hear many sounds that naturally occur in other languages. The tones in the Chinese language are excellent examples of a linguistic blind spot for native English speakers. A Spanish speaker, on the other hand, when first learning English, cannot usually hear the difference
25 between the two English words *beat* and *bit*.
  Since language and culture are intimately bound together, it is not surprising that there are also cultural blind spots. As linguistic blind spots are developed as responses to our early language training, cultural blind spots are developed as responses to our environment.
30 Our culture rewards us for producing certain behaviour patterns and for ignoring others. This training develops in us a cultural perspective by which we judge all acts: a cultural sieve through which we pour all we perceive. Usually this cultural filter performs below the conscious level, producing in us cultural blind spots.
35   We are taught that cleanliness is not only good, but that it is next to godliness. We accept this as a fundamental fact of life and are

quite shocked to discover other cultures that do not. Bargaining in
our culture is not an acceptable way of conducting business, except
in very specific cases, such as buying a house or a car. It bewilders,
40 amuses, or even repels us when we are exposed, in reality or
vicariously, to a Persian market-place.

When a linguistic blind spot is revealed we gain insight into our
own and the target language. We accept this as part of the learning
process. When a cultural blind spot is revealed, we recoil. For most
45 of us the cultural fabric of our lives is so binding that a break from
ethno-centrism is extremely painful. It is the severity of the cultural
change that causes many immigrants to experience cultural shock.

A culture and the language used by it are inseparable. Most of the
cultural attitudes which a native speaker has built into him are
50 reflected in his speech patterns. The reader is invited to consider the
many expressions we have in North American English for talking
about success. We even differentiate between material success,
meaning money, and other forms of success, such as artistic or
moral. The native speaker also brings with him to his language a
55 background of knowledge that is culturally based. We approach the
words 'raw flesh' with a built-in abhorrence. Expressions such as the
'revolution', 'the Indian wars', 'the Great Plains', and 'New York
City' all have a significance to the native American speaker that the
foreign student will not automatically understand or appreciate.
60 Language and culture are connected in several other intimate and
dynamic ways. The language is a product of the culture, but
simultaneously the culture is shaped by how the language allows us
to view it. In English we must view things in some time-oriented
manner. Nothing can exist outside of time, no two activities can take
65 place in the same place at the same time. The backgrounds of most
inhabitants of a culture are similar. A majority of us hear similar
stories when we are young. When we encounter such descriptions as
'as capricious as the Queen of Hearts' or 'like Long John Silver' we
understand the intended reference. The language and culture
70 reinforce each other. The culture begins by giving a viewpoint.
Language gives this idea oral expression, which in turn gives validity
and habit response to the viewpoint.

A cultural pattern is one of these forms that is extremely difficult
to delineate. We have far less trouble in deciding whether or not a
75 specific act belongs to our culture than we do in setting down the
criteria that we use in making such a decision. Given the social
context and the specific act, a native speaker seldom has trouble in
naming the cultural pattern. A man eating bacon and eggs at nine in
the morning we would label as a man eating breakfast, but if asked

to describe the cultural concept 'breakfast' we would probably say 'It depends'.

That would be correct, it does depend. It depends upon the time of day, the type of food being eaten, how many meals had been eaten before, where the meal is being eaten, and many more cultural considerations built into the linguistic form. The cultural concept is the underlying pattern, not the specific act, but the specific act usually contains and reflects all the major elements of the basic pattern. By expanding a specific incident and drawing upon the pupils' experience, you will be able to bring into sharp focus many important areas of our society that are often only on the periphery of the students' understanding.

It is really not difficult to decide what aspects of an act are important and worth teaching and which are not. Ask yourself these two questions:

1   Is this information needed by the students for the proper understanding of the habit and/or concept?

2   Am I, as a native speaker, sure about this detail?

If the answer to either question is No, do not bother about teaching or discussing that aspect of the cultural pattern. In the second question, we are not assuming that you can judge every aspect of our culture. Rather we feel that the students have so many new things to learn and if you got on without that particular knowledge, then surely your pupils will be able to also.

We feel that materials in a language programme should take cognisance of the relationship between culture and language. Using materials that do, the teacher will be able to effectively teach the linguistic items within their cultural context, thus providing not only the patterns of the language but also the trappings that make them meaningful.

J R Gladstone
Language and Culture   (in English Language Teaching XXIII.1 1969) pp 114–117 abridged

1   *'The universe is ordered in accordance with the way we name it.'* (lines 6–7).

   a   According to the author, how are culture and language linked? Do you agree with his point of view?

   b   How is the author using the term 'culture'. Is this how it is commonly used?

   c   Give other examples of the way in which language and culture are linked.

2   The author uses the terms *linguistic blind spots* and *cultural blind spots*.
    a   What does he mean by these terms?
    b   Give other examples of your own.
    c   How do these two terms help us to understand the problems of foreign students?
3   Why does the author say that it is easier to identify a cultural pattern than to define it?
4   How does the author suggest that we should decide what aspects of a specific cultural act should be taught? Do you agree with this approach?
5   According to the author, a language programme should take into account the relationship between culture and language. Examine any coursebook of your own choosing and determine to what extent this has been done.

FOR FURTHER REFERENCE

1   W Rivers   *Teaching Foreign-Language Skills* (University of Chicago Press 1968) Chapter 11.
2   M Finocchiaro   *English as a Second Language* (Regents Publishing Company 1974) pp 94–97   *Developing Cultural Insights.*
3   H C Trivedi   *Culture in Language Learning* (English Language Teaching Journal XXXII.2 1978)
4   B Tomalin   *Teaching about Britain* (Modern English Teacher 5.4 1977 and 6.2 1978).

1.4 Spoken and Written Language

A fundamental distinction has to be made between speech and writing as aspects of language. This view is based on an appreciation of the nature and possible range of grammatical differences deriving from the respective conditions for the production and reception of
5 language.

Main features of speech

a) Speech, as conversation, implies a speaker-listener situation, with alternating roles. Features involved, therefore, are the physical situation and the presence of an observed listener.

10 b) Normal (informal) conversation requires the spontaneous application of language habits.

c) The signalling devices available to the speaker, apart from word and sentence structure, are gesture, stress and intonation.

d) The physical situation and the prompting of questions permit
15 and evoke laconic utterances, e.g. *Fine picture! Rain! The postman! Yes! No! Of course! On Monday! If I can!*

e) The speaker is prone to anomalies of usage which are either peculiar to speech or more characteristic of that medium. There is, first, the interpolation of non-lexical sounds, such as *ah! oh!*
20 *uh! um! 'm'!* and the non-communicative phrases: *Mind you . . ., Well now . . ., Now then . . ., Just a moment . . ., Let me see now . . ., I mean to say . . ., As I was saying . . .* besides superfluous repetitions, all used in lieu of pauses to allow the speaker more time to formulate his thoughts. Then there are such prevalent
25 deviations from assumed norms as changes of word order (e.g. Object-Subject-Verb for Subject-Verb-Object), breaches of concord, misuse of ellipsis, and, under stress of emotion, disjointed or even incoherent utterances.

Main features of writing

30 a) While the writer-reader relationship corresponds to that of speaker-listener as producer and receiver of language, there is no equal social correspondence. In a speech situation there are two or more participants with interchanging roles, but even in

letter-writing or in the novelist's recording of an interior
monologue the process is virtually one-sided.

b)   Writing lacks the direct signalling devices of speech, namely, the
     physical situation as a factor of meaning, and gesture, stress,
     intonation. Punctuation as a signalling device cannot compare
     for effectiveness with the implications of speech modulation. Of
     the few signs it offers for all purposes, only the full stop and the
     question mark may be presumed to indicate grammatical
     distinctions. In consequence, the writer must rely more on
     structural devices and contextual clues.

c)   For language production, an important feature of writing is the
     adequate time afforded for reflection. However spontaneous the
     application of language habits here too, the writing situation, in
     contrast to that of speech, permits attention to formal structure.

Separate treatment is clearly justifiable, for 'while it is possible to
make a description that is valid for both . . . it cannot be assumed
that a statement made about the grammar of written English is valid
for spoken English or the other way round.'
   Nevertheless speech and writing are not fully on a par. It is
unquestionably assumed now that a 'living' language is basically
speech. This assumption derives from appreciation of the social and
dynamic aspects of language. It is speech, not writing, which serves
as the natural means of communication between members of a
settled community, both for the expression of thought and as a form
of social behaviour. Writing is primarily a means of recording
speech, even though it must be acknowledged as a secondary
medium of communication in its own right.

I Morris

The Factor of Purpose in Grammar Teaching (in English Language
Teaching XXI.1 1966) pp 38–39

1   Refer to the features listed below to discuss the main differences
    between speech and writing:
    a   the relationship between the producer and receiver of
        language;
    b   the signalling devices available;
    c   the linguistic devices.

2   Find the examples which the author gives of the following:
    a   laconic utterances;

b non-lexical sounds;
c non-communicative phrases.

Give other examples of your own.

3 Show how *'punctuation as a signalling device cannot compare for effectiveness with the implications of speech modulation'* (lines 38–39).

4 *'An important feature of writing is the adequate time afforded for reflection* (lines 44–45). How does this affect both the production and reception of written language?

5 Assess the significance of the writer's comments for the teaching of:

a speech;
b writing.

FOR FURTHER REFERENCE

1 J Wallwork *Language and Linguistics* (Heinemann Educational 1969) Chapter 2.
2 D Byrne *Teaching Writing Skills* (Longman 1979) Chapter 1.
3 H G Widdowson *Teaching Language as Communication* (OUP 1978) Chapter 3.
4 A Davies and H G Widdowson in J P B Allen and S Pit Corder (Eds) *The Edinburgh Course in Applied Linguistics* Volume 3 (OUP 1974) *Reading and Writing.*

1.5 Grammar and Lexis

What causes us to draw a distinction between grammar and lexis is the variable range of the possibilities that arise at different places in the language.

In some instances we face a choice among a very small number of
5 possibilities. This happens for instance when we have to choose between 'this' and 'that'; or between singular and plural; or between past, present and future; or between positive and negative. There are some places in every language where we have to make such choices; we cannot avoid them or remain neutral, and there is a limited
10 number of possibilities to choose from. Moreover the range of choice is exhaustive: where 'positive' can be chosen, 'negative' is the only possible alternative. There are other places, however, where we are choosing from a very large number of possibilities; we cannot count them, or draw a clear line round them such as will separate
15 what is possible from what is impossible. In a clause which begins 'he was sitting on the . . .', certain items – chair, settee, bench, stool and so on – are quite likely to follow, but very many others are perfectly possible, and probably no two people would agree on the hundred most likely items.
20 This is the basis of the difference between grammar and lexis. Grammar is concerned with choices of the first kind, where there is a small fixed number of possibilities and a clear line between what is possible and what is not. The second kind of choice is the domain of lexis.
25 It is not the case, however, that all choices in language are clearly of one type or the other, closed or open. What we find is really a gradient, or 'cline': that is, there is a continuous gradation in the patterns of formal choice in language. At one end we have a large number of systems interacting with each other in highly complex
30 ways, but with a small number of fixed possibilities in each: here we are clearly in grammar. At the other end, we have open sets, in very simple interrelations with each other but with a much wider range of choice in each, whose limits are hard to define: here we are equally clearly in lexis. But every language has choices which are round
35 about the middle of this cline, where the number of possibilities is limited but large and the interaction of one choice with others is still

fairly complex. Instances of items entering into choices of this intermediate type in English are 'in, at, on, under', 'if, seeing that, provided that, in case', 'often, never, sometimes, always'.

Language, therefore, does not draw a clear distinction between grammar and lexis. In the formal patterns of language, closed systems in complex interrelations, at one end of the scale, shade gradually into open sets in simple interrelations at the other. Linguistics, however, has to draw a line, because these two types of phenomenon need different theories to account for them: that is to say, we cannot account for both patterns of the grammatical type and patterns of the lexical type with the same categories and relations. This has been recognised since the earliest days of linguistics; we take it for granted that we need both a grammar and a dictionary to describe the form of a language, though we may seldom ask how they differ.

M A K Halliday, A McIntosh & P Strevens
The Linguistic Sciences and Language Teaching (Longman 1964)
pp 21–22

1   *'This is the basis of the difference between grammar and lexis'* (line 20).

   a   Explain the distinction which the authors draw between grammar and lexis.
   b   Give other examples of grammatical systems and lexical sets.

2   The authors say that all choices in language are on a 'cline'.

   a   What do they mean by the term 'cline'?
   b   How does it help to explain, for example, the status of prepositions?

3   *'We need both a grammar and a dictionary to describe the form of a language, though we may seldom ask how they differ* (lines 49–51). From your reading of this passage, explain the difference between the two.

4   How is the distinction between grammar and lexis relevant to language teaching?

FOR FURTHER REFERENCE
1   R Quirk   *The Use of English* (Longman 1968).
2   A E Darbyshire   *A Description of English* (Arnold 1967) Chapter 4.

1.6 Register

A dialect is a variety of language distinguished according to the user: different groups of people within the language community speak different dialects. It is possible to recognise varieties of language along another dimension, distinguished according to use. Language
5 varies as its function varies; it differs in different situations. The name given to a variety of language distinguished according to use is 'register'.

The category of 'register' is needed when we want to account for what people do with their language. When we observe language
10 activity in the various contexts in which it takes place, we find differences in the type of language selected as appropriate to different types of situation. There is no need to labour the point that a sports commentary, a church service and a school lesson are linguistically quite distinct. One sentence from any of these and
15 many more such situation types would enable us to identify it correctly. We know, for example, where 'an early announcement is expected' comes from and 'apologies for absence were received'; these are not simply free variants of 'we ought to hear soon' and 'was sorry he couldn't make it'.

20 It is not the event or state of affairs being talked about that determines the choice, but the convention that a certain kind of language is appropriate to a certain use. We should be surprised, for example, if it was announced on the carton of our toothpaste that the product was 'just right for cleaning false teeth' instead of 'ideal
25 for cleansing artificial dentures'. We can often guess the source of a piece of English from familiarity with its use: 'mix well' probably comes from a recipe, although the action of mixing is by no means limited to cookery – and 'mixes well' is more likely to be found in a testimonial.

30 The crucial criteria of any given register are to be found in its grammar and lexis. Probably lexical features are the most obvious. Some lexical items suffice almost by themselves to identify a certain register: 'cleanse' puts us in the language of advertising, 'probe' of newspapers, especially headlines, 'tablespoonful' of recipes or
35 prescriptions, 'neckline' of fashion reporting or dressmaking

28

instructions. The clearest signals of a particular register are scientific technical terms.

Often it is not the lexical item alone but the collocation of two or more lexical items that is specific to one register. 'Kick' is presumably neutral, but 'free kick' is from the language of football. Compare the disc jockey's 'top twenty'; 'thinned right down' at the hairdresser's (but 'thinned out' in the garden); and the collocation of 'heart' and 'bid' by contrast with 'heart' and 'beat'.

Purely grammatical distinctions between the different registers are less striking, yet there can be considerable variation in grammar also. Extreme cases are newspaper headlines and church services; but many other registers, such as sports commentaries and popular songs, exhibit specific grammatical characteristics. Sometimes, for example, in the language of advertising, it is the combination of grammatical and lexical features that is distinctive. 'Pioneers in self-drive car hire' is an instance of a fairly restricted grammatical structure. The collocation of the last four lexical items is normal enough in other structures, as in 'why don't you hire a car and drive yourself?'; but their occurrence in this structure, and in collocation with an item like 'pioneer' or 'specialist', is readily identifiable as an advertising slogan.

Registers are not marginal or special varieties of language. Between them they cover the total range of our language activity. It is only by reference to the various situations, and situation types, in which language is used that we can understand its functioning and its effectiveness. Language is not realised in the abstract: it is realised as the activity of people in situations, as linguistic events which are manifested in a particular dialect and register.

M A K Halliday, A McIntosh & P Strevens
The Linguistic Sciences and Language Teaching (Longman 1964)
p 87–89 abridged

1 Explain briefly, with examples, the difference between *dialect* and *register*.

2 *'A certain kind of language is appropriate to a certain use'* (lines 21–22).

   a Illustrate this statement with reference to two or more registers of your own choice.

   b With reference to the examples you have chosen, decide whether grammatical or lexical features are more important for identifying these registers.

3 The authors observe elsewhere: *'The choice of items from the wrong register, and the mixing of items from different registers are among the most frequent mistakes made by non-native speakers of a language'.*

  a Illustrate this statement with reference to your own experience of teaching (or learning) a foreign language.

  b What steps would you suggest to ensure that learners understand and master the differences between registers?

FOR FURTHER REFERENCE

1 D Wilkins *Linguistics in Language Teaching* (Arnold 1972) pp 136–139.

2 P Strevens *New Orientations in the Teaching of English* (OUP 1977) Chapters 10 and 11.

3 D Crystal and D Davy *Investigating English Style* (Longman 1969) Chapter 3.

4 J Ure *Practical Registers* (English Language Teaching XXIII. 2 and 3 1969).

5 J Roberts *First Steps in Teaching Register* (Modern English Teacher 4.3 1976).

1.7 Semiotics

Semiotics has been defined as the study of the way in which human beings interact using all the communication devices available to them. In semiotics, an act of communication is viewed as the transmission of information from one person to another; but this information is seen as a composite, as a mixture of meanings, deriving from the simultaneous use of some or all of the 'modalities' of communication – taste, smell, touch, sight, and, of course, hearing and voice. In a single act, one might be speaking, making a gesture, using a particular facial expression, and be touching someone; and only by studying the totality of these actions, semiotics claims, can the meaning of the whole event be ascertained. The object of semiotic study is thus to analyse and compare the various patterns of bodily activity which a community systematically and conventionally makes use of in order to communicate.

I think the first point which must be emphasised is that, while some aspects of semiotics have been noticed in the past, teachers generally speaking have quite underestimated the overall complexity of the semiotic situation. To take the case of facial expressions and gestures cited above, it was only when scholars actually tried to write down what people did with their faces and bodies when they communicated with each other, and developed a visual 'kinetic' transcription (analogous to a phonetic transcription of speech), that it was realised just how many and varied these activities are, and how central they are to understanding the meaning of our behaviour. Many of the cues which signal our attitude towards the person we are addressing, or towards the subject matter of our utterance, or even towards ourselves, are visual in character, and are extremely subtle, involving such matters as slight movements of the eyebrows, movement of the nostrils, movement of single fingers in specific directions and so on. Moreover – and this is the important point for the teacher – these cues are not instinctive; they are learned, conventional activities, which vary from culture to culture. Indeed, so complex is this area that it has been given its own label within semiotics – kinesics. It may be a surprise to some to realise that even the distance we stand from people when we are addressing them is to very great extent controlled by specific cultural considerations – for example, in some cultures one is permitted to stand closer to the addressee than in others. These and related matters would be studied under the heading proxemics. Then again, one might consider the various tactile methods of communicating information that societies have evolved: is it conventional to touch on meeting someone, and if so, which part of the body does one use, and where does one touch the other person? Not to follow the expected patterns of behaviour can lead to a great deal of embarrassment, and in some places even danger!

The importance of these matters to the language teacher should be clear. For after all, if a foreigner fails through ignorance to respect a behaviour pattern which the L1 community considers obligatory, then he may well offend the company so much that it will never allow him to use the beautiful pronunciation and syntax which his language teacher had spent so many years lovingly inculcating in him! I am convinced that the reason why so many foreigners get off on the wrong foot when they arrive in a country is because they are ignorant of some of these semiotic patterns. We are all familiar with the cliché which tries to summarise the way in which a language's intonation can subordinate the 'literal' meaning of a sentence: 'It is not what he said, but the way he said it . . .' But what is equally common is the related comment: 'It is not what he said, nor the way he said it, but the way he looked when he said it . . .' Very often, kinesic information overrules the linguistic information in an utterance: visual actions speak very much louder than words or intonation patterns.

This point is usually under-rated or ignored in standard intonation manuals, and in my view is one reason why such linguistic features as intonation are so difficult to teach. It is often said, for example, that the low rising tone in English has a very complex range of meanings. And on looking in the textbooks, one finds that this does seem to be the case: the tone is sometimes interpreted as 'sympathetic, interested, friendly', sometimes as 'grim, warning, unfriendly'. When presented with what is an apparently contradictory state of affairs, then one might well forgive any foreigner who concluded that English intonation was unlearnable. But, of course, this would be a faulty conclusion, the reason being that the different meanings are nothing to do with the low rising tone at all, but are conditioned by different facial expressions. A smiling face, for example, on the utterance 'really' will produce the 'friendly' range of interpretations; a frowning face, on the same contour, will produce the 'unfriendly' range. There will, of course, be cases of ambiguity; but these do not affect the basic principle. When one

30 considers this, and other, examples of a similar kind, it is clear that reference to kinesics, far from complicating the language teacher's job, could at times actually simplify it.

D Crystal
New Perspectives for Language Study 2: Semiotics (in English Language Teaching XXIV.3 1970) pp 210–211

1 *'In semiotics, an act of communication is viewed as the transmission of information from one person to another'* (lines 3–4).

With reference to this statement explain briefly the nature and purpose of semiotic study.

2 *'These cues are not instinctive; they are learned, conventional activities, which vary from culture to culture'* (lines 31–32).

a What are these 'cues' and why are they important?

b Give other examples of conventional behaviour patterns which would be studied through *kinesics* and *proxemics*.

3 *'Visual actions speak very much louder than words or intonation patterns* (lines 61–62).

a Why does the author emphasise this point?

b How does he illustrate it with reference to teaching intonation? Do you agree with his approach? If you disagree, give your reasons.

4 What kind of activities could be used in the classroom to give language learners a better understanding of the 'communication devices' which form part of semiotics?

FOR FURTHER REFERENCE

1 J Laver and S Hutcheson *Communication in Face to Face Interaction* (Penguin 1972) Chapters 3 and 4.

2 M A K Halliday *Language as Social Semiotic* (Arnold 1978).

1.8 Language Acquisition

If we consider the child's acquisition of language between the ages of
about twelve months and five years, the first thing we might observe
is that quantity of language involved is enormous. The child may
well be in contact with language for most of his waking hours. The
5 contact will take different forms. Some of it will be language directed
at the child by other people, particularly parents. A strong effort will
be made to ensure that this language is meaningful to the child. This
may be done by demonstrating relevant objects and actions in the
surroundings, by an intuitive attempt at simplification of the
10 language, or, in the later stages, by actual explanations.

There will be other language that the child is exposed to, in the
sense that it is produced in his presence, but which will not be
addressed to him and most of which will not be meaningful to him,
at least in the early stages of his language acquisition.

15 Finally, there will be language that the child himself produces.
Part of this will be addressed to other people, but it would be a
mistake to think that such language represents all or even most of
the child's language production. At a certain stage in his language
development he is likely to spend many hours in monologue and
20 imaginative dialogue, regardless of whether there is anyone else
present to stimulate him.

There are some other significant factors about the language that
the child is exposed to. In the first place it is, of course, spoken
language. Secondly, what the child hears is also linguistically-
25 uncontrolled language. By this is meant that there is nothing like the
isolation and repetition of a single sentence structure that is
characteristic of much language teaching. The child acquires his
language without having it predigested for him in this way. Adults
do often make the attempt to simplify their language for the benefit
30 of the child, but what they produce remains structurally varied and,
it is sometimes suggested, even makes things more complicated for
the child. One observation that has been made is that the child may
play language games with himself which involve repeating the same
type of sentence perhaps with minimal alterations, and that this does
35 resemble some productive exercises in language teaching.

The language in the child's environment is also uncontrolled in the sense that it is not made up of perfect samples of grammatical speech. Like all natural speech it is subject to many distortions, omissions and inconsistencies. It is never a direct reflection of the somewhat idealised form of language that is described in grammars. In spite of this the child has the capacity to learn from it and to learn to understand it.

A somewhat self-evident point is that the child learns whatever language he is exposed to. Most children are in contact with one language only and, of course, they become monolinguals. It should not be forgotten, however, that where children are brought up in a consistently bilingual environment, they acquire both languages simultaneously, though with some retardation when compared with monolingual children. There is an initial merging of the two languages, but subsequently they are separated and remain functionally quite distinct.

More interesting perhaps than the language to which the child is exposed is his reaction to it. We have already seen that when he is adequately exposed to language he will produce language himself. In part, what he produces is an imitation of what he has heard and this is a process which adults often try to stimulate, but, contrary to what has generally been thought, a good deal of his language production is not imitative at all. Not only does he have the ability to take words and phrases that he has heard and use them in new combinations; he also actually produces pieces of language that he could not have heard from the other people in his environment.

The feedback that is provided by other people does more than simply inform the child whether or not his message is correctly formed. It also demonstrates to him that his language has an effect on the behaviour of others. Rather than being at the mercy of the environment, to some extent, through language, he can bring the environment under his own control. It would be fairly meaningless to say that this motivates him to learn the language. What it does mean is that he is becoming aware of the regulatory function of language. Through language, he learns, his needs can be met. At first the needs will be material, but later they may include the need for information, advice, permission and so on.

As long as adequate exposure to language is provided, the process of language acquisition that has just been described will be followed by all children who do not suffer some physiological or psychological defect. The rates of learning will not be identical, but they will not be wildly different either. By the age of five a substantial proportion of the grammatical system of the language will have been mastered by all children. Given that children may have very different

80 intellectual endowments, it is the similarities not the dissimilarities in their linguistic development that are so striking.

D Wilkins
Second-language learning and teaching (Arnold 1974) pp 26–30
abridged

1 The author mentions three ways in which the child is in contact with language.
   a What are they?
   b Which of these resembles some form of teaching?

2 The author discusses various features of the language to which the child is exposed.
   a What are these features?
   b Do you think that any of these could or should be taken into account in foreign language teaching?

3 How does the child react to the language he is exposed to?

4 The author refers to 'feedback' provided by other people (line 62).
   a What do you understand by this term?
   b How does this feedback help the child to learn language?
   c How does this feedback compare with the kind provided in the foreign language classroom?

5 From your reading of this passage, do you think that first language acquisition provides some insights for foreign language teaching (or learning)? If so, what are they?

FOR FURTHER REFERENCE

1 G D Kennedy in J W Oller and J C Richards (Eds)   *Focus on the Learner* (Newbury House 1973) *Conditions for Language Learning*.

2 V Cook in R Lugton (Ed)   *Towards a Cognitive Approach to Second Language Learning* (Center for Curriculum Development 1971) *The Analogy between First and Second Language Learning*.

3 S Ervin-Tripp   *Is Second Language Learning Like the First* (TESOL Quarterly 8.2).

Section 2
Approaches to Language Teaching

2.1　Why Teach a Foreign Language?

The object in teaching a language, unless it is simply that of getting pupils over an important educational hurdle, is to enable the learner to behave in such a way that he can participate to some degree and for certain purposes as a member of a community other than his own.
5 The degree to which any particular learner may wish to participate will vary. He may seek to read only technical literature, or he may wish to preach the gospel in a foreign country. These varying degrees of participation require different levels of skill in language performance. They also imply some division of linguistic behaviour into
0 different sorts of skill – these different types have conventionally different names: writing, speaking, taking dictation, reading aloud and so on.

Teaching languages is, and always has been, thought of as developing a set of performance skills in the learner, and syllabuses
5 and timetables are often expressed in terms of skills being taught. *Today we'll have a reading lesson. Tomorrow is the conversation class.* If in any discussion of language teaching we talk about developing skills, such as speaking or understanding speech, we are adopting a psychological view of language; we are considering it as a matter of
0 individual behaviour. Whether we consider that behaviour to be a set of habits or possible responses, a body of knowledge, or a set of rules depends upon the particular psychological account that we adopt of the language behaviour of the individual and how it is acquired. It will, for example, determine our attitude to the function
5 and use of drills, the giving of grammatical explanations, the value of repetition and learning by heart, the utility of dictation and the importance of just listening. Whatever decision we make in the field of methods implies the adopting of a view of language as a phenomenon of individual psychology. What characterised so-
0 called 'traditional' language teaching was not so much that it lacked an awareness of the psychological dimension of language, as that it limited the range of behaviour or skill aimed at. But this is not a reason for being critical of it. The skills it attempted to develop were, after all, presumably those which society thought appropriate at the
5 time. Its methods were, in part, determined by this. What one can nowadays justifiably say about 'traditional' language teaching is

that its methods are no longer appropriate to a new set of demands and expectations.

However, when we talk about acceptable or unacceptable be-
40 haviour or appropriate or inappropriate language, we are taking a view of language as a social institution, a body of socially conditioned or culturally determined ways of behaving. What is incorrect or inappropriate is simply that which is not in conformity with the shared norms of a particular group. In language teaching
45 we are preparing the learner to participate in some other social group, some language community other than his own, to play a part or fulfil a role in that community. Unacceptable or inappropriate language prevents him from interacting or communicating satisfactorily with other members of that community; he may fail to achieve
50 his ends, he may fail to communicate or be misunderstood, he may give offence or make himself ridiculous.

Learners do not all have the same social objectives in learning languages. The range of roles they wish to achieve may vary. Few will wish to be poets in the new language community; some may wish
55 to be wives or husbands; most will have to be content to be 'foreigners'. In planning language-teaching operations we must know what social roles are to be aimed at, what personal objectives the learner may wish to achieve. In other words, we have to decide what 'sort' of language to teach him. The concept of 'a language' or
60 'a dialect' is a sociological not a 'linguistic' linguistic one. We teach *a* language, not just *language*.

S Pit Corder
Introducing Applied Linguistics (Penguin Education 1973) pp 27–29

1 a How does the author define the purpose of teaching a foreign language?
  b Do you think that this is an adequate definition? If not, modify it or suggest an alternative definition.
  c The author gives two examples of how a foreign language learner might wish to participate as a member of a community which is not his own. Give some other examples of your own.

2 The author mentions two views of language.
  a What are they?
  b Say how each of these is likely to affect our view of language teaching.

3 The author refers to 'traditional' language teaching. What kind of teaching do you think he has in mind?

4 The author mentions 'a new set of demands and expectations'.

   a What are some of the principal reasons that students today have for learning a foreign language?

   b How can language programmes be planned to take these into account?

FOR FURTHER REFERENCE

1 W Rivers *Teaching Foreign-Language Skills* (University of Chicago Press 1968) Chapter 1.

2 D Wilkins *Second-Language Learning and Teaching* (Arnold 1974) Chapter 4.

3 M A K Halliday, A McIntosh and P Strevens *The Linguistic Sciences and Language Teaching* (Longman 1964) Part 2 Section 7.

4 C Criper and H G Widdowson in J P B Allen and S Pit Corder (Eds) *The Edinburgh Course in Applied Linguistics Volume 2* (OUP 1975) *Sociolinguistics and Language Teaching*.

2.2 Two Approaches to Language Teaching

There are broadly two strategies for setting up the samples on which the learner is to base his own language behaviour. We can either begin with the language broken down into component parts, which are ordered into a pedagogic sequence and fed to the learner one at a
5 time. The learner gradually builds up his store of language. New language always occurs in the context of language that is already familiar. The possible range and variety of language in actual use is only met relatively late in the learning sequence. This is by far the most commonly adopted approach to language teaching. In modern
10 methods the new language either occurs in a succession of structurally analogous but contextually-unrelated sentences, or it is embedded in a specially-written dialogue. In audio-lingual language teaching a new grammatical structure is usually first presented to the learner in a specially-written dialogue. The dialogue, which is
15 normally very short, provides a context for the new structure and the pupil can learn to use it as a response to another sentence with which he will be familiar from previous lessons. Subsequently, the sentence is taken out of the dialogue and through structural drills (pattern practice) the pupil is given intensive opportunity to produce further
20 sentences, identical in structure but varied in vocabulary. In structural or situational language teaching, the new structure tends to be produced initially as an isolated sentence, which is associated with features of the classroom context so that its meaning becomes clear. As in audiolingual teaching, practice takes the form of
25 intensive oral production of further sentences having identical structure to the one that was presented initially. However, whereas in audio-lingual teaching the practice is cued verbally, by use of such techniques as substitution, insertion, expansion and transformation, in situational teaching the cues are usually visual. The teacher
30 manipulates the physical situation or makes use of visual aids as cues for intensive oral production. There is no reason why longer spoken and written texts should not be used, so long as the language within them is carefully controlled, but this is not often done.

The alternative approach would be to let the learner meet a much
35 greater variety of linguistic forms from the beginning, possibly even language that has not been specially prepared for the learner, and

then focus on one or more specific parts of the text for the modelling process to take place. In this case by no means all the language that is encountered by the learner is subjected to techniques that are
40 intended to encourage the process of generalisation. The nearest approach to this in a modern method is found in audiovisual teaching. The approach resembles audio-lingual only in so far as the initial presentation is in the form of a dialogue. But the dialogue, although specially constructed, is intended to resemble a natural
45 conversation much more accurately. It is longer and may contain several new linguistic items. It will inevitably be more varied linguistically. As with situational teaching, a context is provided for the dialogue, usually in the form of a sequence of pictures, each illustrating one of the utterances in the dialogue. The practice that is
50 intended to promote inductive generalisations again involves taking some of the language structures out of their original dialogue context, but instead of having the analogous production based simply on other examples of the very sentence structure that is being learned, it is cued by such processes as question and answer so that
55 the closer resemblance to natural language production remains.

Whereas the former approach, which begins with separate units of language and gradually accumulates them into the larger whole, might be thought of as essentially *synthetic*, the latter, in which the process is reversed, might be termed *analytic*. While the two are
60 conceptually distinct, it is possible for the linguistic organisation of learning to be neither fully synthetic nor fully analytic, although much teaching leans fairly clearly in one direction or the other.

There are reasons why an analytic or synthetic approach might be preferred in specific circumstances. For example, where learners are
65 going to need to use the language for real social communication while they are learning it, there are advantages in basing teaching on an analytic presentation since it permits far greater freedom in the choice of linguistic forms that the learner will meet. On the other hand there are situations (for example where the pupils are young
70 children) where the quantity of unfamiliar language implied in the analytic approach would be quite daunting. In general, however, either approach may lead to successful language learning.

D Wilkins
Second-language learning and teaching (Arnold 1974) pp 72–74

1 *'This is by far the most commonly adopted approach to language teaching'* (lines 8–9).

Explain briefly what this approach consists of.

2 The author describes two methods through which this approach is implemented.

   a What are they?

   b List the main features of each and show how they differ.

3 The author describes an alternative approach to language teaching.

   a How does this differ from the approach previously described?

   b Compare the function of the dialogue in audiovisual and audio-lingual teaching.

4 *'In general . . . either approach may lead to successful language learning* (lines 71–72).

   a What are some of the reasons why one might prefer either an analytic or a synthetic approach to language teaching?

   b Do you think that one approach is essentially better than the other? Give your reasons.

5 Examine any textbook (or textbooks) of your own choosing to see whether the author is following an essentially analytic or synthetic approach.

FOR FURTHER REFERENCE

1 W Rivers *Teaching Foreign-Language Skills* (University of Chicago Press 1968) Chapter 1.
2 J Pride in H Fraser and W R O'Donnell (Eds) *Applied Linguistics and the Teaching of English* (Longman 1969) *Analysing Classroom Procedures.*
3 J Dakin *The Language Laboratory and Language Learning* (Longman 1973) Chapter 2.

2.3 The Audio-lingual Approach

During the past twenty-five years language teachers have seen it as their main task to give their students a knowledge of the formal, structural patterns of the language being taught. As a result, a typical modern textbook provides plenty of practice in the composition of
5 sentences, but gives little systematic attention to the ways in which the sentences are used for the purpose of communication. The assumption is that, once the grammatical system has been learned, the student will know how to put the system to use in producing sentences of his own, without the need for any further instruction
10 Even when attempts are made to make the lesson material more meaningful to students, as when the introduction of new structures is associated with explanatory actions and pictures, the highest priority is given to grammatical criteria, and the artificially-created 'situations' bear little resemblance to natural language use.
15 The so-called audio-lingual method of language teaching depends heavily on the use of intensive oral drills, or 'pattern practice', designed to give maximum opportunity for practising the structures being taught. Such drills are associated with a high degree of control by the teacher. In a typical syllabus the grammatical patterns are
20 presented one by one, and care is taken to allow the learner plenty of time to absorb each new pattern before he goes on to the next. The aim of this type of teaching is the establishment of automatic speech habits. The exercises are repeated until the student can produce the grammatical forms promptly, accurately and with minimum cons-
25 cious thought. There is no doubt that some aspects of language, especially those involving automatic patterns of concord or 'agreement', can be taught very effectively by means of intensive oral drills. Critics of the audio-lingual method, however, have pointed out that students tend to become bored by the incessant repetition of formal
30 patterns, especially if no meaningful purpose is apparent in the exercises. Many drills are designed in such a way that the student is able to produce strings of sounds quite mechanically without a thought for the meaning of what is being said. Whatever the intention of such drills may be, their effect is to encourage students
35 to practise the forms of the language, and to neglect the meanings which ought to be associated with the forms.

As an alternative to pattern-based, habit-formation method, a number of writers have recently proposed a notional or semantic approach to language teaching in which the traditional structural
40 syllabus would be replaced by one based on meaning rather than form. Instead of bringing together sets of grammatically identical sentences, the writer of a notional syllabus would attempt to teach language appropriate to the kind of situation in which the learner is likely to want to use the foreign language. Learning units would
45 have functional rather than grammatical labels; the resulting materials would be functionally unified but grammatically hetero-genous, reflecting how things are in real life where situations do not contain grammatically uniform language. The proposal that text-book writers should pay attention to the context in which language
50 is used is of course not new. Generations of tourists visiting foreign countries have equipped themselves with handbooks in which 'useful phrases' are collected under headings referring to physical situations – 'at the bank', 'at the station', 'at the theatre' – or to types of functional communication – 'ordering a meal', 'buying a suit',
55 'asking the way'. In order to develop a genuine creative use of language, however, the learner must not confine himself to learning forms solely for their value in a single situation. He needs to study not complete situations but the component parts of situations, not complete sentences but the underlying speech acts – denial, disagree-
60 ment, affirmation, approval – by means of which we give expression to our views, and attempt to influence the behaviour of others. The aim of the learner should be, not to learn a series of 'model conversations' off by heart, but to acquire a set of variable strategies which he can employ for himself as the need arises.

J P B Allen
Some Basic Concepts in Linguistics in J P B Allen & S Pit Corder (Eds) *The Edinburgh Course in Applied Linguistics* Volume 2 (OUP 1975) pp 24–26

1 *'The aim of this type of teaching is the establishment of automatic speech habits* (lines 21–23).

   a   What characteristics of this approach are mentioned by the author? Compare these with the description in 2.2.
   b   What criticisms are referred to? Do you agree with them?
   c   Do you think that there is a place in language teaching for intensive oral drills? If you do, mention some of the features of language for which you would wish to use them, giving reasons why you think they are effective.

2 The author describes an alternative to 'pattern-based, habit-formation method'.

    a How does this approach differ from the one described earlier?

    b What special reasons are given for adopting such an approach? Do you agree with them?

3 *'The resulting materials would be functionally unified but grammatically heterogeneous'* (lines 45–47).

The author refers to three types of functional communication: ordering a meal, buying a suit, asking the way. Give examples of the 'heterogeneous grammar' likely to be needed to teach any of these.

4 The author emphasises that language learners need to master 'underlying speech acts – denial, disagreement, affirmation, approval' and 'to acquire a set of variable strategies which he can employ for himself as the need arises'.

From your experience of language teaching (or learning), do you think that these needs are neglected or insufficiently taken care of in 'typical modern' textbooks?

FOR FURTHER REFERENCE

1 W Rivers *Teaching Foreign-Language Skills* (University of Chicago Press 1968) Chapter 2.
2 K Chastain *The Development of Modern Language Skills* (Rand McNally 1971) Chapters 3 and 4.
3 T Grant Brown (English Teaching Forum Special Issue: The Art of TESOL Part 1 1975) *In Defence of Pattern Practice*.

2.4 Teaching for Communication

I should like to consider a problem in the teaching of English which has come into particular prominence over the past few years, and to suggest a way in which it might be resolved.

The problem is that students frequently remain deficient in the
5 ability to actually use the language and to understand its use, in normal communication, whether in the spoken or written mode.

It seems to be generally assumed that the reason for this state of affairs is that teachers do not do their job properly; they do not follow the approach to English teaching which is taught to them in
10 training colleges and on in-service courses, and which is embodied in the prescribed textbooks. The assumption is that if only teachers could be persuaded to put this approach into practice, then the problem would disappear. It is seldom that the validity of the recommended approach is called into question. What I want to
15 suggest is that the root of the problem is to be found, in fact, in the approach itself.

In general, we might characterise the recommended approach as one which combines situational presentation with structural practice. Language items are presented in situations in the classroom to
20 ensure that their meaning is clear, and then practised as formal structures by means of exercises of sufficient variety to sustain the interest of the learner and in sufficient number to establish the structures in the learner's memory. The principal aim is to promote a knowledge of the language system, to develop the learner's com-
25 petence by means of controlled performance. The assumption behind this approach seems to be that learning a language is a matter of associating the formal elements of the language system with their physical realisation, either as sounds in the air or as marks on paper. Essentially, what is taught by this approach is the ability to compose
30 correct sentences.

The difficulty is that the ability to compose sentences is not the only ability we need to communicate. Communication only takes place when we make use of sentences to perform a variety of different acts of an essentially social nature. Thus we do not
35 communicate by composing sentences, but by using sentences to make statements of different kinds, to describe, to record, to classify

and so on, or to ask questions, make requests, give orders. Knowing what is involved in putting sentences together correctly is only one part of what we mean by knowing a language, and it has very little value on its own: it has to be supplemented by a knowledge of what sentences count as in their normal use as a second kind value. What I want to suggest is that the contextualisation of language items as represented in the approach we are considering is directed at the teaching of signification rather than value, and that it is for this reason that it is inadequate for the teaching of English as communication.

The distinction I am trying to make between these two kinds of meaning may be made clearer by an example. Let us suppose that we wish to teach the present continuous tense. The recommended approach will advise us to invent some kind of situation to demonstrate its meaning. One such situation might consist of the teacher walking to the door and saying 'I am walking to the door' and then getting a number of pupils to do the same while he says 'He is walking to the door, They are walking to the door' and so on. Another might consist of the teacher and selected pupils writing on the blackboard to the accompaniment of comments like 'I am writing on the blackboard', He is writing on the blackboard' and so on. In this manner, we can demonstrate what the present continuous tense signifies and we can use the situations to develop 'action chains' so as to show how its meaning relates to that of other tense forms. But what kind of communicative function do these sentences have in these situations? They are being used to perform the act of commentary in situations in which in normal circumstances no commentary would be called for. Contextualisation of this kind, then, does not demonstrate how sentences of this form are appropriately used to perform the communicative act of commentary. What is being taught is signification, not value.

The reaction of many teachers to this observation will be to concede that contextualisation of this kind does not teach what I have chosen to call value, but to assert that in the restricted circumstances of the classroom, this is the only kind of meaning that can be taught. Furthermore, they may feel that it is not necessary to teach value anyway; that the teaching of what I have referred to as signification provides learners with a basic knowledge of the essentials of the language, and that it is a simple enough matter for the learner to put this to use when it comes to communicating. As I have already implied, it seems to me that it is a radical mistake to suppose that a knowledge of how sentences are put to use in communication follows automatically from a knowledge of how

⁸⁰ sentences are composed and what signification they have as linguistic units. Learners have to be taught what values they may have as predictions, qualifications, reports, descriptions and so on. There is no simple equation between linguistic forms and communicative functions. Affirmative sentences, for instance, are not ⁸⁵ always used as statements, and interrogative sentences are not always used as questions. The linguistic form can fulfil a variety of communicative functions, and one function can be fulfilled by a variety of linguistic forms.

What I should like to suggest is that we should consider ways of ⁹⁰ adapting the present approach to the teaching of English so as to incorporate the systematic teaching of communicative value. I would propose that, in the process of limitation, grading and presentation, we should think not only in terms of linguistic structures and situational settings, but also in terms of communicat-⁹⁵ ive acts.

H G Widdowson
The Teaching of English as Communication (in English Language
Teaching Journal XXVII.1 1972) pp 15–18

1 The author refers to a 'problem in the teaching of English'.

  a What is the problem he is referring to?

  b What does he say is generally believed to be the cause of this problem?

2 The author suggests that the root of the problem lies in a particular approach to teaching.

  a How does he describe this approach? Do you agree with his description?

  b What is the weakness of this approach, in the author's opinion?

  c Explain the distinction he draws between *signification* and *value*. Do you agree that this is an important distinction?

3 '*Contextualisation of this kind does not demonstrate how sentences of this form are appropriately used to perform the communicative act of commentary* (lines 64–67).

  a What kind of contextualisation is the author referring to?

  b What alternative forms of presentation for the Present Continuous tense can you suggest which would demonstrate the communicative act of commentary?

4 '... in the restricted circumstances of the classroom, this is the only
   kind of meaning that can be taught' (lines 70–72).
   a In your experience, do teachers restrict themselves just to the
      teaching of *signification*?
   b Do you think that for the teaching of certain items teachers
      might be justified in teaching *signification* at the initial
      presentation stage before concerning themselves with the
      question of teaching *value*? Give your reasons.

5 Examine any textbooks of your own choosing to see what
   opportunities the learners are given for learning the communicative value of linguistic forms. Give particular consideration to the question whether the procedures suggested will work
   with large classes (e.g. of about 30 students).

FUR FURTHER REFERENCE

1 H G Widdowson *Teaching Language as Communication* (OUP
   1978) Chapter 1.
2 S Pit Corder *Introducing Applied Linguistics* (Penguin Education 1973) Chapter 2.
3 JPB Allen and HG Widdowson in JPB Allen and S Pit Corder
   (Eds) *The Edinburgh Course in Applied Linguistics Volume 2*
   (OUP 1975) *Grammar and Language Teaching* pp 86–92.

2.5   Functions, Grammar and Level

To recognise the desirability of a functional approach is not in any way to claim that structural knowledge of the language is unnecessary or unimportant. Grammatical competence is a part of communicative competence, and the language teacher is clearly
5 committed to ensuring that his students are able to manipulate the language structurally (entailing 'grammatical knowledge') as well as use it appropriately (entailing 'functional knowledge'). Given such a commitment, it is relevant to ask to what extent the functional syllabus may provide a suitable framework for tackling the former
10 task.

In a functional syllabus the items to be taught are grouped according to ways in which they may be used, to form units bearing such titles as 'Greetings', 'Making Requests', 'Invitations' etc. We may wish our unit on 'Making Requests' (for example) to introduce
15 exponents such as 'Would you mind opening the window?', 'Could you open the window, please' and 'Open the window, please'. Though these sentences may function in a similar way, they are structurally quite dissimilar; and indeed it seems reasonable to expect sentences which form a homogeneous functional grouping to be grammatically
20 unlike. The choice of a functional organisation therefore seems to imply a degree of structural 'disorganisation' to the extent that many structurally dissimilar sentences may be presented in the same unit, while important examples of sentences having the same structure will be scattered throughout the course.

25 Indeed, it is difficult to impose any kind of structural ordering (or grading) on a functional syllabus. It does not seem to be generally the case that the language used to expound one function is structurally any simpler or more complex than the language used to expound any other. The 'language of greeting' may be as simple or as
30 complex as the 'language of inviting', for example. Hence it is (generally, and with some specific exceptions) impossible to ensure structural progression simply by ordering the units in a particular way. We may be tempted to impose an artificial structural grading (as at times doubtless cannot be avoided), ensuring that grammati-
35 cally complex structures are made to follow structurally simpler ones by careful selection of the exponents to be introduced. But if the materials are to remain functionally accurate, the degree to which

52

this may legitimately be done is clearly restricted; and anyway the resulting structural progression will in no way approach the carefully plotted grammatical grading found in a well-designed structural syllabus.

The course-writer who attempts to reconcile functional organis-ation with structural grading is thus constantly faced with problems of this type: he wishes to introduce the ('complex') structure 'Would you mind opening the window?' in the unit on 'Making Requests'; indeed he feels that to omit such a common form of requesting from the unit would be to commit a functional travesty. Yet this unit occurs early in the course, before other units containing structurally related but 'simpler' sentences such as 'I would like to open the window' (with the 'would' form) and 'I'm opening the window' (with the -ing form). An alternative to functional travesty is to switch unit order; but this creates other equally serious structural anomalies, since every unit introduces a number of exponents of varied structural complexity.

Structural practice within a functional design is of course possible. After the introduction of 'I haven't seen you for 3 weeks' in a unit on 'Greetings', for example, one strategy would involve the teacher interrupting the (functional) flow of the lesson to provide a grammatical explanation – a difficult and lengthy task, however, unless students are already familiar with present perfect and time constructions using 'for'. A structural drill may even be given, though if the functional organisation is to be maintained, one might argue that examples which are not associated with greeting (but which may nevertheless be grammatically crucial examples) will have to be excluded. Given that the sentence is but one of a number of structurally heterogeneous exponents introduced in the unit, the teacher will also be forced by time constraints into a selection of grammar points for detailed treatment which will almost certainly exclude many sentences deserving equally thorough consideration. Add to this the fact that the course design may provide little opportunity for follow-up work – the next example of present perfect + for may occur some 10 units later – and it becomes clear that, though grammatical practice may indeed be given within a func-tional framework, it is difficult to focus attention on structural concerns in a principled or comprehensive way.

Where such concerns are felt to be important, a functional design might better be avoided. High intermediate or advanced students, already familiar with much of the language's grammar, need not suffer from the lack of an organised and graded structural presen-tation – for such students it is a case of re-presentation, rather than

initial introduction, of grammatical structures. They will most certainly benefit from the focus on language use afforded by a functional syllabus design, and this may enrich their previous language-learning by providing an important 'functional
85 dimension'.

It might be convincingly argued that at the elementary level a degree of attention should be paid to structural considerations that cannot easily be given within the framework of a functional syllabus. The future may clarify which of a number of possible strategies is
90 suitable: a grammatical approach at the lower levels followed by a functional approach for more advanced students may indeed prove to be the optimal solution. The student would progress from learning how the language operates to learning how it is used, utilising grammatical and functional syllabuses respectively to focus
95 on each task. On the other hand, time may provide evidence that the advantages of presenting language as a system of communication through a functional syllabus may, even at an elementary level, justify the unordered grammatical presentation (which, after all, a child acquiring its first language successfully learns to cope with). In
100 this situation we might legitimately begin to speak of a 'functional method' on a par with audio-visual, audio-lingual and other methods. A third possible solution would indicate that a mixture of structural and functional approaches at the elementary level – with grammatically orientated (components of) units following func-
105 tional (components of) units – might prove to be efficient.

These remain speculations, however, and where one is concerned not with experimental applied linguistics but with syllabus design affecting the future language-learning experience of large groups of students, there seems no responsible alternative to confining the use
110 of functional syllabuses in general courses to the non-elementary levels. At the beginner stage teachers should be sceptical of 'abandoning the partly negotiable currency of the grammatical approach for the crock of gold at the end of the functional rainbow'.

K Johnson
The Production of Functional Materials (in ELT Documents (The British Council 1976/1)) pp 19–20

1 *'It is difficult to impose any kind of structural ordering on a functional syllabus'* (lines 25–26).

a Explain the reason for this.

b From what the author says, why should this be desirable?

54

2 *'Structural practice within a functional design is of course possible'* (lines 55–56).
   a What possibilities are suggested?
   b What are some of the difficulties involved?

3 a What conclusion does the author reach about the application of a functional approach to language teaching? Do you agree with him?
   b In your opinion, has he given a balanced assessment of the problem involved? Give your reasons.

4 Examine any coursebook which implements or claims to implement a functional approach to language teaching at the beginning stage to see whether the author has attempted to maintain some kind of structural progression. Decide whether he has successfully resolved the issues raised in this passage by the author.

FOR FURTHER REFERENCE

1 D Wilkins *Notional Syllabuses* (OUP 1976).
2 K Johnson *Syllabus Design and the Adult Beginner* (Modern English Teacher 6.2 1978).
3 C Silva *Recent Theories of Language Acquisition in relation to a Semantic Approach to Foreign Language Teaching* (English Language Teaching Journal XXIX.4 1975).

2.6 The Role of Situational Teaching

Perhaps it is not unreasonable to suppose that the presentation of language in situational dialogues is as old as formalised language-training itself. The approach persists in modern courses for reasons which are too obvious to need stating. It has served as the only
5 effective antidote to the surfeit of tedious mechanistic drilling, which, unfortunately, is considered by some teachers to be the be-all and the end-all of language-teaching. Course-designers have almost universally superimposed two important refinements on this traditional device: audiovisual presentation and grammatical con-
10 textualisation. The situations in many published courses are designed with visual presentation in mind and they generally illustrate quite well the use of the grammatical item(s) to be taught in the grading sequence. Beyond this, perhaps it is fair to say that the technique has not been further developed. Indeed, the situations
15 devised by course-writers are often at variance with the needs of the learner. Consider, for instance, the emphasis on some kind of story-line in adult courses in which the situations are wholly irrelevant to the concerns of the student, dealing with such unlikely topics as (say) a woman quarrelling with her mother-in-law in a Hampstead flat. Or
20 consider the rather random situations which are generated by a close adherence to a structural sequence. Even practical situations (buying railway tickets and so on) are often presented on the demonstrably false assumption that the student will be able to function in precisely the same way when he finds himself in similar
25 circumstances. What is generally lacking is an underlying rationale for the construction of situations in terms of student needs.

Before attempting to assess the role of situational teaching we must draw a clear distinction between situations as they occur in real life and situations which are fabricated for language teaching
30 purposes. The former can never be adequately defined, for they embrace the sum total of human activity; the latter need to be defined fairly precisely, given the accepted limitations of any published course. Situations which will be suitable for language teaching purposes must subsume a variety of factors which will vary in
35 accordance with the level and age-range the course is geared to. These factors may be itemised as follows:

Function: The broadly-defined language act which is to be taught: e.g. apologising.

Notion: The general and/or specific application of the function: e.g. apologising for failing to meet you at the station.

Topic Area: The subject-matter to be dealt with derived from such general themes as the family, the home, work, entertainment, travel, etc.

The Setting: The precise location which provides the general physical background of the situation. Setting may be concrete or non-specific.

Interaction: How the speakers are communicating (politely, impolitely, formally, informally, etc.) and what it is they are talking about.

Social Role: The relationship between the speakers (buyer/seller; colleague/colleague; husband/wife; native/non-native, etc.)

Exponents: The utterances (sentences, patterns, idioms, interjections, structural and lexical items) which stem from the factors itemised above.

In real-life situations, these factors often combine in unpredictable ways and are further complicated by facial expression, gesture, body-attitudes, inflexion, often incoherent and unfinished utterances, while a whole range of functions (surprise, anxiety, warning, anger, relief) may be deployed in rapid succession as the situation develops and unfolds. In a language course, the range of reference is far more modest and is deployed to one end only; to facilitate language-acquisition. We must always be aware of the difference between the unprocessed language used in real life and the processed language employed in a course. It may be that ultimately the student will reach a sufficiently high level in L2 to respond intuitively to all the complexities and nuances of a real-life situation and to manipulate a wide range of communicative strategies, but this can only be considered an ultimate goal which is attained by relatively few learners. With reference to syllabus construction, we must draw a distinction between 'desirable objectives' and 'practical objectives'. 'Desirable objectives' are the specifications covering functions, notions, topic areas and exponents which might reasonably be assembled by some general body (e.g. an examination board). It is up to the individual course-designer to derive practical objectives (i.e. the blueprint for a course) from such general specifications.

L G Alexander
Some Basic Assumptions Affecting Course Design (in English
Language Teaching Journal XXX.2 1976) pp 95–97

1 'Course-designers have almost universally superimposed two important refinements on this traditional device' (lines 7–9).
  a What is the 'traditional device' that the author is referring to?
  b Explain the two 'refinements' that course designers have
     superimposed.

2 'The situations devised by course-writers are often at variance with
   the needs of the learner' (lines 14–16).
   What criticisms are made of situations in published materials?
   Do you agree with them? Give your reasons.

3 The author lists the following factors which must be taken into
   account in language teaching situations:
     – function
     – notion
     – topic area
     – setting
     – social role
     – exponents

  a Reread lines 37–55 and then explain, without further reference
     to the text, what is meant by each of these.
  b Taking the function of *making requests* (referred to in 2.5),
     suggest how these factors might be taken into account in
     devising a situation to present this function.

FOR FURTHER REFERENCE

1 J Van Ek *The Threshold Level for Modern Language Learning*
   (Longman 1976).
2 K Morrow *Teaching the Functions of Language* (English
   Language Teaching Journal XXXII.1 1977).

Section 3
The Organisation of Learning

3.1 Aims and Objectives

My purpose is to draw a distinction between aims and objectives in language teaching: to suggest, as a matter of practical usefulness (1) that the term aims be reserved for long-term goals such as provide the justification or reason for teaching second languages and (2) that objectives be used only for short-term goals, such as may reasonably be achieved in a classroom lesson or sequence of lessons. Neglect of this distinction is more than a matter of mere terminology, since it tends to blur the very real difference between, on the one hand, teaching approach and on the other hand lesson content.

Teacher approach is something which is (or should be) largely governed by the long-term aims of the course. Thus a language course for students who merely wish to acquire a reading knowledge of a foreign language will not require the same approach from the teacher as a course which aims at enabling the student to acquire proficiency in conversation. In the former case, the teacher will concentrate above all on the receptive skills of reading (rather than on the receptive skill of listening or the productive skills of speaking and writing, although these three cannot be entirely ignored even in a reading course). Thus the long-term aim of the course dictates the teacher's approach, but not the content of any particular lesson. Lesson content is a matter of the immediate objectives to be achieved within the lesson. Thus, in the above example, within a general framework of concentration on reading skills (dictated by the aims of the course) the teacher will want to lay down, as precisely as possible, the immediate objectives to be attained within the lesson – precisely which items of written language are to be read and learned (in terms of words, structures, etc.). By clearly stating his lesson objectives (in his lesson notes), he will not only be very clear in his mind about what he wants to teach, but will have a corresponding concern to ensure that these particular items are learned by the class.

Writers on methodology are well aware of the harmful confusion which results from failure to distinguish between what I have termed aims and objectives. Thus Mackey, in discussing syllabus content, asks:

> 'What objectives does the syllabus include? The most usual are: understanding, speaking, reading, writing, grammar,

translation, acquaintance with the history, civilisation and literature of foreign peoples, better understanding of the native language, mental discipline, social adaptability, and
40 use of foreign discoveries. The list is typical of many a syllabus which makes no distinction between reasons for teaching a second language and the objective to be achieved. Such reasons as the understanding of foreign civilization are listed together with reading ability under the general heading
45 of "aims".'

Mackey here uses both the terms which I am discussing, i.e. objectives and aims. However, he does not define these terms, although he does clearly make a distinction between reasons for teaching a second language and the objectives to be achieved. In his
50 terminology 'understanding foreign civilisations' is given as a reason for teaching, and 'reading ability' is, by implication, considered an objective of teaching.

Mackey is here complaining of the confusion which results from lumping reasons and objectives together as 'aims'. What Mackey
55 means by reasons for teaching are in fact the long-term goals of language teaching, for which I have suggested that we should reserve the term 'aims' as a contrast to 'objectives' (immediate lesson-goals). The use of separate terms ('aims/objectives') not only provides a convenient indication of whether we are discussing short-term or
60 long-term goals, but also helps to clarify what items can suitably be included under the two heads.

R Roberts
Aims and Objectives in Language Teaching (in English Language
Teaching Journal XXVI.3 1972) pp 224–227

1 a What distinction does the author make between aims and objectives?
  b Why does he regard this distinction as important? Do you agree with him?
  c How does he illustrate the distinction between aims and objectives?

2 The author quotes from W F Mackey on syllabus content. How could the latter part of the passage (beginning: *The List is typical . . .*) be rephrased to incorporate the author's distinction between aims and objectives?

3 Later in his article the author quotes the following list of aims from W Rivers (*Teaching Foreign-Language Skills*):

(i) to develop the student's intellectual powers through foreign-language study;

(ii) to increase the student's personal culture through the study of the great literature and philosophy to which it is the key;

(iii) to increase the student's understanding of how language functions and to bring him, through the study of a foreign language, to a greater awareness of the functioning of his own language:

(iv) to teach the student to read the foreign language with comprehension, so that he may keep abreast of modern writing, research, and information;

(v) to bring the student to a greater understanding of people across national barriers by giving him a sympathetic insight into the ways of life and ways of thinking of the people who speak the language he is learning;

(vi) to provide the student with skills which will enable him to communicate orally, and to some degree in writing, with the speakers of another language and with speakers of other nationalities who have also learned this language.

a Which of these aims are also referred to by Mackey?

b Which of these aims are generally stressed in current syllabuses and course books?

FOR FURTHER REFERENCE

1 W F Mackey *Language Teaching Analysis* (Longman 1965) pp 323–333.

2 W Rivers *Teaching Foreign-Language Skills* (University of Chicago Press 1968) Chapter 1.

3 G Perren *Specifying the Objectives* (English Language Teaching XXV.2 1975).

4 D Wilkins in E R Bauer (Ed) *Teaching Languages* (BBC 1976) *Objectives and Methods*.

3.2 Lesson Planning

It is essential that the teacher should know for every moment of the lesson exactly what he is expecting every pupil to be doing, and of course what he should be doing himself. Whether the work is silent, like reading or writing, or controlled oral activity at class or group
5 level, or free group activity, the teacher should know exactly what kind of behaviour he is expecting from the class, and how that relates to the teaching aims of the lesson. This means that, at the beginning of his career, the teacher will certainly need to spell out in great detail the aims of the lesson and the activities which will help to realise
10 those aims. If the teacher starts by doing a training course which provides teaching practice, there is usually time to prepare lessons in detail and to consult with tutors and fellow-students, so that the process of preparation is developed carefully and systematically. But not all teachers are lucky enough to be able to do this.
15 Nevertheless, in the early years of teaching such careful preparation is essential, and some teachers prefer to work as carefully throughout their working lives.

This means that a lesson plan is likely to contain several different types of information, which need to be clearly distinguished. First, it
20 will contain the main points in the organisation of the lesson for the benefit of the teacher; then it will also contain detailed organisational information about class activities; finally it may contain a great deal of 'content' material which the teacher cannot expect to remember – like the detailed forms of oral exercises, or a passage to
25 be read to the class, or a list of points which will be put on the blackboard for a writing exercise. A good lesson plan will not mix up these different types of information, but will lay them out so that the teacher can use them easily in class without the class being aware that notes are being consulted all the time.
30 An example of a workable lesson plan is given on page 65.

It will be seen from the lesson plan that the teacher has two main aspects to consider: the selection of materials, and the choice of classroom procedures. The problems of the selection of materials relate partly to the overall level of the class and the nature of the
35 school's syllabus or scheme of work, but they also relate partly to the classroom procedures which are used.

AIMS =
A LANGUAGE =

1. Revise 'giving directions'
2. Punctuation of direct speech via picture story

B INTERACTION — 3. Pair practice = fluency

TAKE IN

Direction cards
Plan of 'Balloon dialogue'   Pictures in textbook
Pictures and story

	Teacher	Pupils
I	(a) ASK 3 pupils 'How can I get to the football pitch, please?' + chemistry lab. secretary's office	Listen and answer if asked
approx. 10 mins	(b) GIVE OUT DIRECTION CARDS EXPLAIN = work in pairs, like last week GO ROUND GROUPS	Work in pairs with cards
II not more than 10 mins	(a) TELL picture story and WRITE dialogue on board	Listen
	(b) Quick DRILL of story (as on attached sheet)	Choral and individual
5 mins	(c) ORGANISE pupils in threes – 2 to retell story and other to check: then move around	Work in threes
5-10 mins	(d) TELL to write story rapidly 5 mins (COLLECT DIRECTION CARDS WHILE THEY WRITE)	write
	(e) TELL to check for punc- tuation of speech in pairs NB Ask me if there are problems	Check in pairs
10 mins +	(f) (if time) – go through in class	

When teaching large classes, particularly, the teacher has to think carefully about the most appropriate ways of enabling *every* pupil to participate as fully as possible in the lesson. In planning his teaching, he has to decide at each stage on the answers to two main questions. The first is – Do I want the class to be doing exactly the same piece of work at the same time? and the second is – Do I want them all to be working as one group, centred on me or the blackboard, or do I want them to be working in a number of independent groups? These are not two versions of the same question: there will be many occasions when the class may usefully work in small groups, all simultaneously practising the same piece of language or preparing the same piece of written work.

G Broughton et al.
Teaching English as a Second Language (Routledge and Kegan Paul 1978) pp 178–180.

1 *'In the early years of teaching . . . careful preparation is essential'* (lines 15–16).

   a Why is lesson planning essential? Do you think it is possible to teach well without a lesson plan?

   b Suggest what can be learnt from the *experience* of preparing lesson plans.

2 Look at the lesson plan on page 65.

   a What different types of information does it contain?

   b Does this lesson plan seem to you to be workable? If not, what modifications would you suggest?

   c It is sometimes suggested that lesson plans should be written out on filing cards. What advantage do you see in doing this?

3 With reference to a unit in any coursebook with which you are familiar, prepare a lesson plan or series of lesson plans to show how the unit can be broken down into a number of workable stages.

FOR FURTHER REFERENCE

1 K Chastain *The Development of Modern Language Skills* (Rand McNally 1971) Chapter 12.

2 M Finocchiaro *English as a Second Language* (Regents 1974) pp 49–52.

3 E D Allen and R M Valette *Modern Language Classroom Techniques* (Harcourt Brace 1972) Appendix. (Note: the lesson plans are for German, Spanish and French).

4 J Haycraft *An Introduction to English Language Teaching* (Longman 1978) Chapter 12.

3.3 Stages of Teaching and Learning

A teacher presenting a new grammatical point, for example, can adopt one of two techniques: demonstration or involvement. In either case he wants to give the pupils examples of the new structure or rule. He can demonstrate its meaning by presenting the examples in isolation or, at the most, in contrast with something already known but easily confused. Both the isolation and the contrast are intended to call the pupils' attention to the novelty of the point. The teacher is saying in effect: 'Here is something new'. He hopes to make its meaning clear by mime, pictures, or translation, or by providing a minimal context.

If he prefers the technique of involvement, he will not tell the pupils that he is going to use a new structure, but will slip examples of it into something else he is saying in such a way that it will be understood and accepted quite naturally. The past tense, for example, can be unobtrusively but appropriately introduced in telling stories to the class. The teacher can sometimes even get the pupils to 'invent' the structure themselves. A class of children involved in drawing or painting, for example, will sooner or later demand more paper or more paint. At this point, when the demand is freshly felt but as yet unexpressable in the new language, the teacher can slip onto the tips of the pupils' tongues such structures as 'I want X', or 'Can I have some more Y?'.

Demonstration and involvement both require interaction between teacher and pupils. Having presented examples of the new structure or rule, the teacher must now go on to *practise* it. This means getting the pupils to produce their own examples in response to some question or cue. The techniques of practice, as they are practised in the classroom, once again require interaction between teacher and pupils. The teacher listens to what the pupils say, approving or emending, and the pupils have to note both the teacher's cues for the next response and his reactions to the last one. Where there is a breakdown in their responses, the teacher can present the point again or give further examples. He can also provide explanations in the new language or, if need be, in the mother tongue. At this stage, and in the next one, a pupil's actual responses are often unexpected or confused. He may have difficulty in formulating the new structure or he may betray that he has misunderstood its meaning.

The next stage is *development* where the teacher has to relax
40 control over the pupils' performance. The pupils are set tasks such as telling a story themselves, describing pictures, retailing their daily lives and past or future activities, expressing their own needs and preferences. The successful completion of such tasks calls for the use not only of the structure that has just been practised but of all that
45 has been learnt before. The teacher cannot and should not interrupt the pupils' performance by correcting every single mistake. He can indicate that he does not understand, he can prompt where the pupil falters and he can override him when he pauses for breath, but many slips made in the flow of utterance can only be dealt with later, if at
50 all. The stage of development thus involves its own kind of interaction between the pupil and his audience – the interaction of real conversation – but for the first time the pupil can select the cues to which he will respond. As far as organising and developing his own utterances is concerned, he is largely on his own.

55 When the teacher comes to formally *testing* what the pupils have learnt, he must relax control altogether and leave the pupils entirely on their own. This is essential if the test is to be a fair one of what has been learnt, what still needs to be learnt, and what has to be taught again.

60 Let us take a closer look at what the pupil is doing while the teacher is busy presenting, practising, developing and testing. In the last two stages, I have suggested that the pupil is increasingly on his own. But surely he is always on his own? We may teach a class, but each pupil has to learn for himself. If we look at the whole teaching
65 process from the pupil's point of view, we can see that it also falls into four stages, each corresponding to the changing intentions of the teacher.

When the teacher presents the new point, the pupil has to understand it. When the teacher practises the point, the pupil has to
70 learn it. And when the teacher seeks to exploit the newly acquired knowledge, the pupil has to control it. As we have seen, any developmental task may call upon all that he has already learnt. In addition, it requires him to express himself not just correctly, but well.

For the pupil, if not for the teacher, testing is a continuous
75 process, co-extensive and co-terminous with everything he does. Each effort to understand tests his intelligence and his knowledge of the language. Each effort to speak tests his memory of the rules and his ability to apply them in response to new cues or new situations. As long as he has the teacher's attention, he can immediately find out

whether he is right or wrong. Formal tests, however, have little extra value for the pupil, though they may stimulate him to learn. For a formal test cannot usually be allowed to give the pupil immediate and detailed information about how well he is doing.

To summarise and contrast what has been said about the stages of
5 learning and the stages of teaching, every step in the teaching process requires continual interaction between teacher and pupil, while every step in the learning process requires continual effort on the part of the pupil.

J Dakin

The Language Laboratory and Language Learning (Longman 1973)

pp 4–6

1 The author identifies four stages of teaching.

   a What are the four stages?

   b Say briefly what the teacher and the learner have to do at each of the four stages.

2 At the presentation stage the teacher 'can adopt one of two techniques'.

   a What are these techniques and how do they differ?

   b In your opinion, is either of these two techniques more effective? Give your reasons.

3 At the practice stage, the teacher must get the pupils to produce their own examples. Suggest some of the ways in which the teacher can:

   a provide 'cues' – other than questions – to elicit responses from the pupils;

   b help the pupils if they are unable to respond.

4 At the development stage the teacher has to relax control over the pupils' performance.

   a What activities does the author suggest for this purpose? Suggest others of your own.

   b Why does he advise against correcting 'every single mistake' at this stage? Do you agree?

   c How does 'interaction' between the teacher and the pupils at the development stage differ from that at the practice stage?

5 Explain how testing may be regarded as 'a continuous process'.

6 Do you think that the author has provided a useful framework

for looking at the teaching/learning process? In particular, assess its relevance to:

a understanding pupils' needs;
b lesson planning.

FOR FURTHER REFERENCE

1 D Girard *Linguistics and Foreign Language Teaching* (Longman 1972) The four phases of a language lesson.
2 D Byrne *Teaching Oral English* (Longman 1976) Chapter 1.
3 P D Smith *Towards a Practical Theory of Second Language Instruction* (Centre for Curriculum Development 1971) pp 31–34.
4 K Morrow *The Presentation Stage Revisited* (Modern English Teacher 6.4 1978).

3.4 How People Learn

1 *Work out objectives in advance*

Planning a step-by-step course is made much easier if objectives are worked out first (and finalised after the initial meeting with the new class). Try to avoid thinking vaguely in terms of worthy 'aims'. Be absolutely specific and write it all down on paper. What standards do you expect your students to have reached by the end of the course? For instance, which sentence patterns will they be able to use confidently? What size vocabulary will they have? What expertise in accent do you hope for? What will they know about the country whose language they are acquiring? How much speech will they be able to comprehend and how much to speak themselves? Working out precise objectives like this has many advantages. First, it helps to plan the syllabus. It can also be given to students in advance. Perhaps most important, it helps both students and teacher assess their progress.

2 *Work from the known to the unknown*

This advice seems so obvious that it hardly seems worth saying, but teachers sometimes forget to apply it. Generally speaking, we learn new skills by absorbing them into the old. The more connections we can see between the familiar and the unfamiliar, the easier we find it to learn. Here, then, is another reason for finding out what students already know. A simple, friendly form circulated in advance or at the first class will be an immense help. Some students will know a lot, some may never even have heard of verbs, nouns and adverbs. Some may think they know a lot, but may actually know little. Some may be familiar with the country whose language they are acquiring, others not at all. In any case it is important to establish realistic starting points.

3 *Work in short, simple, logical steps*

Knowledge of a subject has a way of becoming a seamless garment when you know enough to be able to teach it. The more expert you become, the harder it is to remember what it was like to know nothing, and the more difficult it is to unpick the different components of the skill. Nevertheless, it must be done. Start with a

few of the simplest structures or words and build on those, adjusting the pace as necessary. It is always safer to have modest objectives for each class meeting and to concentrate on those, for instance, on making sure that every student really understands how to ask the
40 way, how to greet people or how to apologise. It will be immediately obvious if students have thoroughly learnt something: indeed in this case they may eagerly urge you on to the next process. Whereas students who have not understood are often unwilling to admit it, and may simply stop coming to the class in case their ignorance is
45 exposed.

4 *Encourage learning by activity: let learners learn at their own pace*

It is surprising how much education of all sorts still trundles along on the 'hole-in-the-head' theory. This is the one where teachers behave as if they thought students had a space in their heads which
50 could be filled simply by pouring knowledge inside. Such teachers may teach energetically away without their students learning anything. Most of us have experienced the results of this method when we sit through lectures with politely interested expressions on our faces while our minds are busily engaged elsewhere. Learning is
55 not a passive process. If students are to learn, they must be actively engaged in doing, not just listening but comprehending.

In language classes, this will mean each student spending a maximum of time using new vocabulary, speaking, listening to and reading the language. Most students will greatly prefer this anyway,
60 after they have overcome their initial reticence. It is a waste of time and money for a student to come to a class and then only speak one or two hesitant sentences: he would be better off with a good home study course borrowed free from the library!

Most students will make much greater progress if they work
65 individually, in groups or pairs on materials the teacher has already prepared. The whole group can be kept together for the relatively rare occasions when discussion or a talk is the appropriate method.

Students often relish working through a 'problem-solving' or discovery approach. Some students may be disconcerted not to be
70 spoonfed, but the majority respond to opportunities for working out basic principles, doing projects and research and other similar activities which fully engage their intelligence and interest.

5 *Success*

People learn most quickly when they get a right answer to a problem.
75 The feeling of achievement is one of the best possible spurs to wanting to continue learning. It is commonly said that 'we learn by

our mistakes'. In reality, people thrive on success: it is much more difficult to profit from failure. This does not mean letting mistakes go uncorrected. It does mean designing tasks which are just within each learner's competence so that the possibility of making errors is absolutely minimal, while the task itself is just complex enough to retain his interest. A mistaken first attempt has a way of fixing itself permanently in the learner's mind.

Giving success and achievement is especially vital at the first class meeting. Even a small piece of language successfully understood sends people away feeling that they have spent their time usefully and eager to return for more. Always offer praise if possible (nothing fulsome: a simple nod or smile will often do). It is important here to distinguish between effort and achievement. In our achievement-dominated world, we often overprize the actual end-product, ignoring the considerable effort that may precede it.

6 Give 'feedback'

It is difficult to learn anything unless you know how you are getting on. For instance, you are unlikely to be able to improve your own teaching unless you get 'feedback' on your performance from your students and your boss. Sometimes of course, this is of a rather crude and unhelpful kind: students may stop coming to your class without telling you why. Some teachers, however, learn to improve their teaching by carefully scanning their students (a slumped body usually means a slumped mind), by encouraging criticism and by asking a more experienced tutor to sit in with them. This way, in the jargon, they get 'knowledge of results', or 'feedback' and can try to capitalise on their strong points while minimising the weak ones. In the same way, students need some way of assessing their own progress. The simplest way is for you to make detailed comment straightaway on written or spoken work. Other possibilities are 'self-checking devices', where the student checks his response for himself against an 'answer' column.

7 Give practice and reinforcement

It is easy to plough on with a prepared syllabus and to forget that students must keep on practising to reinforce the skills they may have somewhat shakily acquired. In most of today's language courses this is no problem: the later parts of the course naturally keep on reinforcing earlier ones.

J Rogers
Adults as Learners and Classroom Management (in *Teaching Languages* BBC 1976) pp 25–28 abridged

1 The author discusses how people learn under the following headings:
   (i) Work out objectives in advance
   (ii) Work from the known to the unknown
   (iii) Work in short, simple, logical steps
   (iv) Encourage learning by activity: let the learners learn at their own pace
   (v) Success
   (vi) Give 'feedback'
   (vii) Give practice and reinforcement

   State briefly what advice the author offers in connection with each of these.

2 Give your own views on the following:
   a   The more connections we can see between the familiar and the unfamiliar, the easier we find it to learn (lines 20–22).
   b   Learning is not a passive process (lines 54–55).
   c   Most students will make much greater progress if they work individually, in groups or pairs on materials the teacher has already prepared (lines 64–66).
   d   People learn most quickly when they get a right answer to problem (line 74).
   e   Students need some way of assessing their own progress (lines 104–105).

3 Do you think the author gives a reasonably adequate guide to how people learn? If not, say what additional or alternative advice you would offer.

FOR FURTHER REFERENCE

1 M Finocchiaro   *English as a Second Language* (Regents 1974) pp 37–39.
2 A Howatt in JPB Allen and S Pit Corder (Eds)   *The Edinburgh Course in Applied Linguistics Vol 3* (OUP 1974) *The Background to Course Design.*

3.5 Motivation

Psychologists have distinguished two major attitudinal factors which play an important role in determining how willing the learner is to persevere with the task. On the one hand, there are foreign language learners who view the language as a key to social and cultural enrichment through the opportunities it provides for association with members of a different culture. This type of *integrative* motivation is characteristic of many successful language learners. Really wanting to be able to learn the foreign language as a means for close communication and acceptance by people who speak it provides the will power necessary to persevere with the task. Good motivation leads not only to perseverance but to a heightened concentration or intensity of attention that produces more rapid learning. On the other hand, the learner may simply be studying the language for an immediate short-term goal which does not involve his wanting to be accepted by and integrated into a target culture group. Simply learning a language to acquire course credits, or to carry out a limited range of tasks that do not involve the learner in close face-to-face interaction as an equal (for example, a taxi driver learning enough English to collect tourists at an airport) does not generally lead to a high degree of accomplishment in learning. Foreign language or second language learning in such cases is typically poor, characterised by acquisition of only the rudiments of grammar and by tolerance of a relatively low standard of achievement.

This type of attitudinal contribution to second language learning is not of course under the control of the teacher, although he may be able to encourage and influence an integrative motivation towards the target language group. But there are also the day-to-day activities of classroom language learning and it is in those that the teacher's contribution to the motivational dimension can be important. The classroom teacher is faced with the problem of trying to guide the learning process so that at every step the learner is motivated through the satisfaction of achievement, but at the same time perceives the need for further progress. The actual experience of learning a foreign language, however, is often a disillusioning one because of the unrealistic assumptions about language learning

which learners hold when they begin. The student who expects to be able to converse with ease after three months of study may be bitterly disillusioned to find that the acquisition of conversational
40 skills is more likely to take thirty months of intensive practice. The student who wants only a reading knowledge of the foreign language will find that the effort to build up a basic recognition vocabulary of 5,000 to 7,000 words is considerable, and even then in reading he may encounter six to ten words per page that he does not know.
45   Many conventional language teaching techniques likewise are not likely to sustain any but the most devoted student in the arduous learning task. Some language teaching textbooks continue to be teacher-oriented, planned in terms of 'items' and 'teaching points'. Often the long-term aims of the textbook writer, based on his
50 syllabus of structural and lexical items, ignore the short-term realities which face the learner in the day-to-day classroom routine. A half-century ago, Palmer, one of the founders of British language teaching theory, noted that the tendency among educators of the day was towards 'methods involving the intelligent use of the
55 intelligence, methods which develop the reasoning capacities, methods which form judgment. Geography is no longer a process of learning lists of place-names by heart, history is no longer represented as a catalogue of dates, arithmetic is taught by playing with cubes.' Palmer rejected this movement as irrelevant to language
60 teaching, because he did not see such methods leading toward automatism and habit formation. The view of language as a *habit* rather than a *process* has tended to have an inhibiting effect on the development of language teaching materials and has led to a proliferation of techniques and methods based on memorisation
65 and repetition. More recent views on language have led to the investigation of teaching techniques which more directly involve the learner in communicative tasks, problem solving and information seeking. These techniques require the learner to utilise the language creatively as an instrument of learning. The additional motivation
70 generated by such procedures is said to make learning more meaningful and effective.

J C Richards

Second Language Learning in R Wardaugh and H D Brown (Eds) *A Survey of Applied Linguistics* (University of Michigan Press 1976) pp
131–133

1   The author refers to two kinds of motivation.
   a   What are they?

b   How does each affect attitudes towards language learning?

2   *'The actual experience of learning a foreign language . . . is often a disillusioning one.'* (lines 34–35).

   a   What examples does the author give of 'unrealistic assumptions' that learners make? Can you give other examples of your own?

   b   What steps could be taken to avoid situations like the ones he mentions?

3   The author criticises certain conventional language techniques.

   a   What kind of techniques does he have in mind?

   b   Why does he criticise them? Do you agree with his criticisms?

   c   What alternative techniques does he suggest? Why are they likely to be more effective?

4   Give your own assessment of the importance of motivational factors in language learning and say what steps you would take to ensure that learning is meaningful and effective.

FOR FURTHER REFERENCE

1   R C Gardner in J W Oller and Jack C Richards (Eds) *Focus on the Learner* (Newbury House 1973) *Attitudes and Motivation: Their Role in Second Language Acquisition.*

2   A N Smith *The Importance of Attitude in Foreign-language Learning* (English Teaching Forum Special Issue: The Art of TESOL Part 1 1975).

3   P Mugglestone *The Primary Curiosity Motive* (English Language Teaching Journal XXXI.2 1977).

4   R L Allwright *Motivation – The Teacher's Responsibility* (English Language Teaching Journal XXXI.4 1977).

5   B and P Goodman-Stephens *Motivation: A Practical Guide* (Modern English Teacher 5.4 1977).

3.6 Teaching Pupils How to Acquire Language

Teachers have always been concerned with facilitating learning, sometimes with more intervention, sometimes less. The teacher should not control his class in the sense of pre-arranging everything that is uttered, but he should control it to the extent of knowing – as
5 far as the current state of knowledge allows him to – why he has organised it in the way he has, and by permitting freedom only within the framework of what is known of the language-learning process. For example, group discussion can be very free or it can be very restricted; in both cases it can be very valuable – but it is not
10 valuable *because* it is group activity, it is valuable because of the changes which it contributes to producing in the learner, and if the teacher has no idea what sort of changes he is hoping to produce (i.e. no analytical framework of language functions or language forms related to the learner's needs), he has no way of distinguishing
15 learning activity from non-learning activity (or activity which contributes to learning other, irrelevant or even harmful things) and no way of talking to fellow-workers about what he is doing and thus of improving and learning himself. Ultimately, the classroom can only be a 'free' class within a definition which the teacher under-
20 stands of what the purpose is of that freedom. The function of research and discussion is to make that definition as explicit as possible so that the teacher can operate in the light of the best available understanding – but it is the teacher who operates; he cannot avoid being central and however freely the pupil may appear
25 to be operating, it will always be within a tacit framework of what the teacher has allowed. For this reason, it seems more sensible to concentrate not on the *extent* of teacher intervention but on the *nature* of teacher intervention. Teacher intervention cannot be withdrawn, but it can be modified, and its characteristics can be described with
30 greater or less explicitness.

It would seem, then, that the discussion of language teaching may be best couched in the form: 'Given the learner is like *this*, the teacher should organise things like *this*'. As we are increasingly able to understand new aspects of the language-learning process, so our
35 understanding of the role of the teacher will change. However, as our discussion focuses more and more on the learner, there is a

danger that a number of distinctions which are frequently made will tend to be confused with each other, and I would like, briefly, to try to keep them apart.

1 *Arbitrary language use versus 'real' language use:* except for the language of class organisation and control, language used in the classroom will always be arbitrary, selective and unspontaneous, simply because classrooms are places organised for ends beyond themselves. Nonetheless, it is possible to minimise the arbitrariness by means of (e.g.) simulation exercises, discussion, overt teaching of other subjects, etc. The question here for the teacher is: How close can my teaching take pupils to their anticipated language needs in the outside world?

2 *Language use versus language practice:* there are many ways of using language in the classroom, but it has to be remembered that while all language use is language practice, not all language practice is language use. In fact, this distinction is really a version of the accuracy-fluency division, for language practice is all too often only concerned with the accuracy of phonological or syntactic patterns. The question for the teacher is: How much opportunity am I giving members of my class to talk as individuals to each other, using as much English as they can, to say things which they have decided to say and which are as far as possible in response to what has been said before – practice for fluency rather than accuracy?

3 *Teacher-selected versus pupil-selected items:* there will clearly be a strong tendency for the teacher to select many practice items, but even here it is possible for some degree of pupil freedom to be encouraged, particularly in choice of content words at the early stages. Question: How many times have members of my class determined the wording in practice items?

To summarise the position so far, then. It is suggested that the teacher cannot avoid taking responsibility for the extent and nature of the language work going on in classes under his guidance. The search for 'real' language is misplaced, as scarcely any classroom language is 'real', because classrooms are concerned with equipping people for the world outside: there must always be a willing suspension of disbelief. However, the teacher does need to ensure that practice in fluency (rapid, natural production and reception of contextualised, meaningful language) is provided as much as practice in accuracy. For this to take place, a considerable part of the responsibility for the content of language work must be placed on the

79

pupil, and this responsibility should be given even from the very earliest stages. If this position is accepted as valid for the language-
80 learning situation right from the very beginning, it presupposes a number of techniques for use in the classroom which are not currently accepted in many places at the moment. Some of the most important implications are considered below.

1 Pupils should be given plenty of opportunity to make mistakes. If
85   there is going to be genuinely fluent practice, many mistakes of phonology, syntax and semantics will be made. To demand simultaneous accuracy and fluent production is to demand the impossible for many students. For this reason teachers need to become aware of the relative significance of various kinds of error.
90   Errors will show the teacher the kinds of problem the learner is facing and overcoming, but it must be recognised that some problems are more serious than others. For example, we accept a great deal of variety in pronunciation in native speech and are more tolerant of pronunciation variation from foreign speakers
95   than we are of syntactic variation, though even here we accept variation far more readily in speech than in writing. Bearing in mind the purpose of the utterance, and whether it is spoken or written, the teacher should be prepared – at certain times – to tolerate a wide range of possible mistakes of accuracy in the
100   interests of developing fluent production and comprehension.
2 In the early stages of language learning it may be better to have talk going on in the mother tongue, or in a mixture of mother and English, than to have no fluent talk going on at all. This is not always possible when there are mixed language groups, but –
105   when fluency is the aim of the exercise – any way of promoting frequent and rapid exchange should be encouraged.
3 Pupils should sometimes be given a moment to think about what they are going to say, so that they can contribute meaningfully to the activity. Even at a very early stage, most patterns can be
110   extended by pupils themselves so that they are making true statements about themselves:

        Tomorrow I'm going to . . .
    or   Every day I . . .

Even filling in slots like this will require a little thought, and specific
115 time (a minute or two) should be given for pupils to do their thinking.
4 Pupils' utterances in class should be practised in pairs wherever possible, with all the pairs in the class talking simultaneously. This

means that the pupil-improvised utterance should be followed by some more or less appropriate response. To use the example given in 3 above:

P1: Tomorrow I'm going to . . .
P2: {Oh, aren't you lucky. (depending on the
     {Oh, bad luck.   place being visited)

Responses of this kind are not difficult to set up and, although strongly controlled, they do give an early chance for pupils to produce language which is (a) true, (b) their own in part, and (c) capable of producing a response dependent on the meaning of what they have said.

Pair-work of this kind might only take 20 seconds before the teacher moves on. With larger material for improvisation and more complex exercises, group or pair discussion – relatively uncontrolled – may go on for an hour or more and be very fruitful. But it should be remembered that the teacher is usually tempted, especially at the beginning, to let it go on for too long. It must not reach the point of being unproductive – but we also need to be much clearer than we have been in the past about what constitutes productive language work.

CJ Brumfit
Teaching Pupils to Acquire Language (in ELT Documents (The British Council 1976/3)) pp 25–27

1 *'Teachers have always been concerned with facilitating learning, sometimes with more intervention, sometimes with less'* (lines 1–2).

   a What is the author's view of teacher control in the classroom?
   b Do you agree with his point of view? Give your reasons.

2 The author refers to a number of distinctions which are likely to be confused.

   a What are these distinctions and why are they likely to be confused?
   b How does his 'question for the teacher' help in each case to keep these distinctions apart?
   c Do you agree that these are important distinctions? Give your reasons.

3 The author refers to a number of techniques which he says are not always accepted.

a What are these techniques and what is their overall purpose?
b Do you agree that these are 'valid for the language-learning situation right from the very beginning'? Give your reasons.

4 *'Pupils' utterances should be practised in pairs wherever possible'* (lines 116–117).

Suggest other exchanges which would fulfil the conditions listed in (a)–(c) (lines 125–128).

5 Do you think that the author has given a balanced assessment of the teacher's role in the classroom?

FUR FURTHER REFERENCE
1 W Rivers and M S Temperley *A Practical Guide to the Teaching of English* (OUP 1978) Chapter 1.
2 G Broughton et al. *Teaching English as a Foreign Language* (Routledge & Kegan Paul 1978) pp 76–88.
3 D Byrne *Teaching Oral English* (Longman 1976) Chapters 1 and 7.

3.7 Error Analysis

All learners make mistakes. This is not confined to language learners. We all make mistakes when we are speaking our mother tongue. They often cause a certain amount of merriment. Whether we bother to correct ourselves or not seems to depend on whether we
5 think our hearers have noticed, and how urgently we want to get on with what we are saying. The important point for our present purpose is that we know how to correct them; we can recognise our own mistakes for what they are. This is not usually the case with mistakes made by a learner. Not only does he not always recognise
10 his mistakes, but when his attention is drawn to them he often cannot correct them; he may even commit another error in trying to do so. Furthermore, the majority of learners' errors are linguistically quite different from those made by a native speaker.

We judge a foreigner's knowledge of our language by the number
15 and sort of mistakes he makes. We are inclined to think he knows our language quite well if he does not make many mistakes. It does not usually occur to us that he may be avoiding taking risks and confining himself to doing only what he knows he can do right. The layman probably assesses a foreigner's ability in his language in the
20 first place by how haltingly he speaks and by how good his pronunciation is, that is, in linguistic terms, but in its most superficial aspect. He tends to assume that one can equate a poor pronunciation with a general lack of knowledge of the language, and that a halting speech is confined to those who do not know the
25 language well. The first judgement is without foundation; the second has some truth. However, these superficial judgements are usually revised after a longer exposure to the foreigner's speech. A person more experienced with foreigners knows that a good pronunciation does not necessarily go along with the ability to express oneself
30 fluently or communicate readily in a foreign language. He also knows that fluency is a quality which varies both in foreigners and native speakers with the speech situation and the topic of conversation.

Whilst the nature and quality of mistakes a learner makes provide
35 no direct measure of his knowledge of the language, it is probably the most important source of information about the nature of his

83

knowledge. From the study of his errors we are able to infer the nature of his knowledge at that point in his learning career and discover what he still has to learn. By describing and classifying his
40 errors in linguistic terms, we build up a picture of the features of the language which are causing him learning problems. In this respect the information we get is similar to that provided by contrastive analysis. Error analysis thus provides a check on the predictions of bilingual comparisons, and inasmuch as it does this, it is an
45 important additional source of information for the selection of items to be incorporated into the syllabus.

The most obvious practical use of the analysis of errors is to the teacher. Errors provide feedback, they tell the teacher something about the effectiveness of his teaching materials and his teaching
50 techniques, and show him what parts of the syllabus he has been following have been inadequately learned or taught and need further attention. They enable him to decide whether he can move on to the next item on the syllabus or whether he must devote more time to the item he has been working on. This is the day-to-day value of errors.
55 But in terms of broader planning and with a new group of learners they provide the information for designing a remedial syllabus or a programme of re-teaching. The matter, however, is not quite as simple as this. As we shall see, there is no clear sense in which we can say that a feature or element in the language has been learned
60 completely until the whole language has been learned. If we remember de Saussure's words that language is a 'self-contained system', in which each part is related systematically to another part, then the learning of some new item requires the relearning of all the items already studied; hence the necessity in language learning of a
65 cyclical syllabus.

S Pit Corder
Introducing Applied Linguistics (Penguin Education 1973) pp 256–257 and 265

1 *'We judge a foreigner's knowledge of our language by the number and sort of mistakes he makes* (lines 14–15).

What sort of superficial judgements are often made about a foreigner's language ability? Do teachers sometimes make similar judgements?

2 The author says that errors are probably the most important source of information about the nature of the learner's knowledge of the language.

a Explain both the general value of error analysis and its particular value for classroom teaching?

b To what extent do you think that error analysis is a new development in language teaching?

3 Suggest how error analysis can help us to take a more sympathetic view of language learning problems.

FOR FURTHER REFERENCE

1 W R Lee in H B Allen and R N Campbell (Eds) *Teaching English as a Second Language* (McGraw Hill 1972) *The Linguistic Context of Language Teaching.*

2 D Wilkins *Linguistics in Language Teaching* (Arnold 1972) pp 190–206.

3 A R B Etherton *Error Analysis: Problems and Procedures* (English Language Teaching Journal XXX.1 1977).

4 B Jenner *Error Analysis* (Modern English Teacher 5.2 and 5.3 1977).

5 S Pit Corder in J P B Allen and S Pit Corder (Eds) *The Edinburgh Course in Applied Linguistics Volume 3* (OUP 1974) *Error Analysis.*

6 J C Richards (Ed) *Error Analysis* (Longman 1974).

3.8 Accuracy versus Fluency

As soon as we begin to analyse what we mean by 'knowing a foreign language', we are faced with a host of difficult decisions. Does 'mastery' mean the ability to talk, read and write like a native speaker in any situation? Or does it mean something less than this
5 and, if so, what is the criterion of success? Clearly, in order to answer these questions we must return to the learner's purposes in acquiring the language. For instance, it may be sufficient for a pupil to understand the language over quite a wide range of topics, without being able to produce very much. On the other hand, an ability to
10 speak the language may be more important than an extensive reading knowledge. We cannot decide how much to include in the materials for a course unless we know how much the pupil is expected to recognise in reading and listening.

We must also consider the question of performance standards. If
15 the pupil is expected to be completely accurate, he will obviously learn less in a given time than he would if he were working to a less demanding (and perhaps more useful) criterion, e.g. fluent intelligibility.

Many features of the grammar and pronunciation of a foreign
20 language carry little, if any, semantic information. Verb endings, case inflexions, gender distinctions, prepositions and many spelling rules can all be inaccurately deployed without affecting intelligibility. Of course such errors are irritating and must be dealt with if the learner's ultimate aim requires accurate performance, for
25 example, if he wishes to teach the foreign language. It is, in the end, a matter of priorities: do we want an emphasis on fluency in the early stages which will probably result in inaccuracies but which will provide the learner with a useful command of the language relatively quickly, or do we want slower progress with stress laid on accurate
30 performance of new points as they turn up in the course? It is tempting to go for the latter aim, particularly if one believes that inaccuracies tolerated early in learning will be more difficult to deal with later on. However, it is noticeable that, even if the teaching is very precise and careful, the pupils find it extremely difficult to
35 achieve a high standard of accuracy in the details of the language,

particularly if they have little semantic content. *I go yesterday* is comprehensible enough, after all.

It is very important not to attach irrelevant value-judgements to the two different approaches by thinking of one of them as 'disciplined' and the other as 'slapdash', for example. This misrepresents the whole issue, which is basically one of timing. If our aim is fluency we can let the pupil go on as fast as possible in the beginning stages, aiming only at a reasonably confident comprehension and production of the foreign language in spite of inaccuracies in semantically unimportant rules such as gender, declension, conjugation, etc. Then at a later stage we can take up the details and train a more correct performance. If we do this, there will be certain consequences. Firstly, some pupils will leave the course before the question of detailed accuracy has been seriously raised. Their performance will be faulty, but at least it should be useful. Secondly, the pupils may resist the teacher's attempts to enforce accuracy because it temporarily slows up their fluency of expression. Finally, there may be a problem of 'unlearning' points which have been allowed to pass without much comment in the past. If one believes very strongly that language learning is essentially a matter of habit formation, then this argument is likely to carry a great deal of weight. It should be remembered, however, that inaccuracies persist even with the most stringent teaching methods. This suggests that there is a 'natural' timetable for learning a foreign language just as there undoubtedly is for learning one's native language. The utterances of small children are full of inaccuracies if measured against the standard of developed speech and for the most part they go unchecked because they are not thought of as inaccuracies but as 'underdeveloped speech'. However, if a six-year-old still talks like a three-year-old, then his behaviour does not match the expectations of society, and he will be given special attention of some sort.

If we adopt the more usual aim of accurate performance, one advantage is immediately obvious: the pupils can be examined and tested to see whether they have acquired this accuracy or not. Accuracy is simple to examine, because it tests grammatical rules which can be easily judged right or wrong, and so tests can be marked without too much argument. Fluency is almost impossible to mark fairly, which is a pity because it is a more important skill in most real-life situations. The second consequence of an accuracy-dominated approach is that some pupils leave the course before they have learnt enough of the foreign language to be of much practical use. There is only a limited amount of time at the teacher's disposal in any teaching situation. If he spends that time insisting on accuracy

in all the details, he will obviously not have time to train a fluent,
80 more wide-ranging command of the language.

Faced with a choice between accuracy and fluency, most teachers will naturally tend towards a compromise position: as much accuracy and as much fluency as possible in the time available. However, teaching systems being what they are with their inevitable
85 demand for testable behaviour from the pupils, the accuracy criterion is almost bound to find favour with the majority of teachers. In fact the problem goes deeper than this. Fluency in the early stages of learning is very difficult to recognize. After all, if a student has not learnt very much, he cannot easily demonstrate how
90 good he is at expressing his ideas. Accuracy, however, is very easy to recognise, with the result that an inaccurate learner is a very much louder comment on the teacher's skill than an inarticulate pupil.

A Howatt
The Background to Course Design in J P B Allen and S Pit Corder
(Eds) *The Edinburgh Course in Applied Linguistics Volume 3* (OUP
1974) pp 16–18

1 *'It is, in the end, a matter of priorities'* (lines 25–26).

   a   What are the main arguments for and against placing greater
       emphasis in the early stages of language learning on
       (i) accuracy; (ii) fluency?

   b   Which point of view do you agree with? Say why.

2 The author cites *'I go yesterday'* as an example of the kind of
   mistake which language learners easily make.

   a   Is this the kind of inaccuracy which you would tolerate, even
       if greater priority were being given to fluency? Give your
       reasons.

   b   Give examples of other errors which you think should be
       tolerated in the early stages of language learning.

3 Examine any recently published coursebook for the beginning
   stage and decide whether the author is mainly concerned with
   promoting accuracy or fluency.

FOR FURTHER REFERENCE

1 C J Brumfit *Teaching Pupils to Acquire Language* (ELT Documents The British Council 1976/3).

3.9　The Purpose of Testing

Before we can even begin to plan a language test, we must establish its purpose or function. Language tests have many uses in educational programmes and quite often the same test will be used for two or more related purposes. The following list summarises the chief objectives of language testing; the categories are not by any means mutually exclusive, but they do indicate six different emphases in measuring student ability or potential.

1　To determine readiness for instructional programmes. Some screening tests are used to separate those who are prepared for an academic training programme from those who are not. Such selection tests have a single cutoff point: examinees either 'pass' or 'fail' the test, and the degree of success or failure may not be deemed important.

2　To classify or place individuals in appropriate language classes. Other screening tests try to distinguish degrees of proficiency so that examinees may be assigned to specific sections or activities on the basis of their current level of competence. Such tests may make no pass-fail distinctions, since some kind of training is offered to everyone.

3　To diagnose the individual's specific strengths and weaknesses. Diagnostic screening tests generally consist of several short but reliable subtests measuring different language skills or components of a single broad skill. On the basis of the individual's performance on each subtest, we can plot a performance profile which will show his relative strength in the various areas tested.

4　To measure aptitude for learning. Still another kind of screening test is used to predict future performance. At the time of testing, the examinees may have little or no knowledge of the language to be studied, and the test is employed to assess their potential.

5　To measure the extent of student achievement of the instructional goals. Achievement tests are used to indicate group or individual progress toward the instructional objectives of a specific study or training programme. Examples are progress tests and final examinations in a course of study.

6 To evaluate the effectiveness of instruction. Other achievement tests are used exclusively to assess the degree of success not of individuals but of the instructional programme itself. Such tests are often used in research, when experimental and 'control'
40 classes are given the same educational goals but use different materials and techniques to achieve them.

For simplicity, the foregoing six categories can be grouped under three headings: aptitude (category 4 above), general proficiency (categories 1 to 3), and achievement (categories 5 and 6). These three
45 general types of language tests may be defined in the following manner:

An aptitude test serves to indicate an individual's facility for acquiring specific skills and learnings.

A general proficiency test indicates what an individual is capable
50 of doing now (as the result of his cumulative learning experiences), though it may also serve as a basis for predicting future attainment.

An achievement test indicates the extent to which an individual has mastered the specific skills or body of information acquired in a formal learning situation.
55 Not all measurement specialists use this three-way division of tests or interpret the terms aptitude, proficiency and achievement precisely as we have done above. Our three categories do, however, seem to lend themselves well to the classification of language tests and will be of value in helping to differentiate among the principal
60 testing objectives.

D Harris
Testing English as a Second Language (McGraw Hill 1969) pp 2–4

1   The author identifies three general types of language test.
    a   What are they and what is the purpose of each type of test?
    b   How do these three types of test relate to the six functions of testing which were discussed earlier?

2   Do you think it would be preferable to use the term *assessment* for any of the purposes the author describes? Give your reasons.

3   Assess the importance of these different types of test for:
    a   the classroom teacher;
    b   the learners.

FOR FURTHER REFERENCE

1   A Davies (Ed)   Language Testing Symposium (OUP 1968).

2 J P B Allen and A Davies   *Testing and Experimental Methods* in *The Edinburgh Course in Applied Linguistics Volume 4* (OUP 1977).

3 E Ingram in J P B Allen and S Pit Corder (Eds)   *The Edinburgh Course in Applied Linguistics Volume 3* (OUP 1974) *Language Testing.*

4 R L Cooper in H B Allen and R Campbell (Eds) *Teaching English as a Second Language* (McGraw Hill 1972) *Testing.*

5 G Perren   *Testing Ability in English as a Second Language* (English Language Teaching XXI.2, XXI.3 and XXII.1).

6 I McGrath in S Holden (Ed)   *Teacher Training* (Modern English Publications 1979) *Testing: what you need to know.*

3.10 Testing for Communication

To what extent should we concentrate on testing the student's ability to handle elements of the language such as phonology, vocabulary and grammar and to what extent should we concentrate on testing the integrated skills? Our attitude towards this question must
5 depend on both the level and the purpose of the test. If the testee has been learning English for only a relatively brief period, it is highly likely that we shall be chiefly concerned with his ability to handle the language elements correctly. Moreover, if the aim of the test is to sample as wide a field as possible, a battery of tests of the language
10 elements will be useful not only in providing a wide coverage of this ability but also in locating particular problem areas. Tests designed to assess mastery of the language elements enable the test writer to determine exactly what is being tested and to pre-test items, carrying out statistical analyses to determine the degree of reliability and later
15 revising them where necessary.

However, at all levels but the most elementary, it is generally advisable to include test items which measure the ability to communicate in the target language. How important, for example, is the ability to discriminate between the phonemes /iː/ and /i/? Even if
20 they are confused by the testee and he says: Look at that sheep sailing slowly out of the harbour, it is unlikely that misunderstanding will result because the context itself provides other clues to the meaning. All languages contain numerous so-called 'redundancies' which help to overcome problems of this nature. Furthermore, no
25 student can be described as being proficient in a language simply because he is able to discriminate between two sounds or because he has mastered a number of structures of the language. Successful communication in situations which simulate real-life is the best test of mastery of a language. It can thus be argued that fluency in
30 English – a person's ability to express facts, ideas, feelings and attitudes clearly and with ease, in speech or in writing, and his ability to understand what he hears or reads – can best be measured by tests which evaluate performance in the language skills. Auditory and reading comprehension tests, oral interviews and essays assess
35 performance in those language skills used in real life.

Too great a concentration on the testing of the language elements may indeed have a harmful effect on the communicative teaching of the language. There is also at present insufficient knowledge about the weighting which ought to be given to specific language elements. How important are articles, for example, in relation to prepositions or pronouns? Such a question cannot be answered until we know more about the degrees of importance of the various elements at the various stages of learning a language.

J B Heaton
Writing English Language Tests (Longman 1975) p 6

1 The author refers to *'testing the student's ability to handle elements of the language'* (lines 1–2).

At what level and for what purpose does he suggest that it is appropriate to test this kind of ability? Do you agree?

2 *'Successful communication in situations which simulate real-life is the best test of mastery of a language* (lines 27–29).

   a Why does the author argue that we should pay special attention to measuring communication ability?

   b Do you agree with the kind of tests he suggests? Give your reasons.

3 What special problems are likely to be encountered in attempting to measure communication ability?

FOR FURTHER REFERENCE

1 J Upshur *Objective Evaluation of Oral Proficiency* (English Teaching Forum Special Issue: The Art of TESOL Part 2 1975).

2 J W Oller in J W Oller and J C Richards (Eds) *Focus on the Learner* (Newbury House 1973) *Discrete Point Tests versus Tests of Integrative Skills.*

3 J W Oller *Language Tests at School* (Longman 1979).

Section 4
Skills in Language Learning

4.1 Speech and Writing

In the field of foreign language teaching there has been a tendency to advocate the primacy of speech over writing as a general educational goal. Generally speaking, it is sound practice, particularly in the early stages of learning a language, to give first priority to the development of automatic speech habits. The aim of oral drill is to develop the student's capacity for immediate and spontaneous assimilation of complete speech units. Students must be prevented from developing what Palmer calls the 'isolating habit'; he must be made to 'think the whole sentence integrally' instead of piecing it together bit by bit while he is saying it. However, a number of arguments that have been advanced in support of teaching the oral skills first appear to be based on questionable assumptions. Typical arguments in favour of speech before writing are: it reflects the way children learn their native language; writing is only an imperfect representation of speech, and involves extra problems of orthography; the transfer in learning from the spoken to the written form is greater than the reverse. On closer examination it appears that all these arguments are open to question. Because speaking before writing is the natural order in first language learning, it is not necessarily the only, or the most advantageous, order in second language learning. The spelling system of English, which is often characterised as highly arbitrary and confusing, in fact contains a variety of useful morphological information which is not present in the acoustic signal. Finally, there has never been any convincing demonstration that students transfer more easily from speech to writing than the other way round. In fact, most adult students find it easier to understand and retain what is orally presented if they are able to refer to written notes. As far as we can tell, this does not prevent them from achieving oral fluency so long as they do not become overdependent on the written symbol.

The view that spoken language has priority and that writing is a secondary reflection of speech, to be practised only when the speech patterns have been well established, is particularly prejudicial to the teaching of writing in a foreign language. The principle of speech before writing may be justified at the beginning of a syllabus, when the aim is to establish a basic vocabulary and the essential sentence patterns as quickly as possible, but as soon as students have progressed beyond the elementary stage it becomes obvious that writing is a skill in its own right which owes little to the inculcation 40 of patterns of speech behaviour. It is virtually impossible by means of oral drill alone to elicit the complex patterns which are a commonplace in writing and which have to be mastered if a student wishes to write effectively. If we want to teach advanced students how to write in a foreign language we must find some ways of 45 promoting composition as an end in itself and not simply as an adjunct to speech.

J P B Allen
Some Basic Concepts in Linguistics in J P B Allen and S Pit Corder (Eds) *The Edinburgh Course in Applied Linguistics Volume 2* (OUP 1975) pp 26–27

1 To what extent does the author support the principle of teaching speech before writing? What are his reasons and do you agree with them?

2 The author lists some typical arguments which are used in support of teaching speech before writing.
a What are these arguments?
b On what grounds does the author question them?
c What is your own view?

3 From your own experience of teaching or learning a foreign language say whether you think that access to the written form hinders oral fluency.

4 *'Writing is a skill in its own right'* (line 39).
a What conclusions does the author draw from this statement? Do you agree with them?
b Examine any coursebook at the post-elementary level to see whether writing is treated as a skill in its own right.

FOR FURTHER REFERENCE

1 D Wilkins *Second-language learning and teaching* (Arnold 1974) pp 61–65.
2 D Byrne *Teaching Writing Skills* (Longman 1979) Chapters 1–3.

4.2 The Importance of Receptive Skills

Interestingly, modern methods are notably alike in the extent to which they require the productive participation of the learner in the learning process. This stems partly from a reaction against the somewhat passive role of the learner in traditional teaching, but more from the belief that learning only takes place when the learner himself is active. Since, at the same time, receptive abilities are erroneously thought of as passive, the demand for active participation becomes a demand for the learner to engage principally in the production of language. Materials are planned so that each newly-introduced linguistic form, be it a grammatical structure or a lexical item, is thoroughly practised by the learner. Practised here means that he himself is given repeated opportunities to produce the form – orally, because of the simultaneous emphasis on speech. To make this possible there is a strict limit on the number of new forms in any learning unit, so that the burden of what must be covered productively is not too great. It is often the case that everything that is learned at what may be roughly labelled the elementary and intermediate levels is learned for production.

As might be expected, the results of this productive emphasis in the method will be a strengthening of productive skills and a weakening of the receptive skills, although it should not be forgotten that the exact nature of the achievement will depend on the exact nature of the experience. Even intensive oral practice may not provide all that is necessary for a mastery of spontaneous oral production.

There are two reservations about the role given in current language teaching to productive language activities. First, all language knowledge is tied to what there is time to produce in the classroom. This does not reflect in any way either the normal balance of our language knowledge or the relationship between production and comprehension in language acquisition. This constraint is quite unnecessarily and damagingly artificial. The fact that comprehension can develop ahead of production is something that should be recognised and exploited in language teaching. As it is, it tends to be suppressed in the belief that it is confusing for the learner to be in contact with forms that are not fully within his productive repertoire.

Since this is an inevitable part of anyone's day-to-day language experience, it is better that the learner should be prepared for it.

The second reservation is that limiting the learning experience to production guarantees a very slow and thin exposure to language. Language acquisition is based on a rich, varied and intensive contact with language. In language learning the time available for contact is already considerably reduced. If we insist too much on language production, because this requires maximal repetition of specific linguistic forms, we offer a still weaker exposure to language even within the learning time available. If we give a larger place to receptive activities, not only do we ensure that the receptive abilities themselves are better learned, we give the learner the opportunity to learn what is not taught. In language learning a rich exposure to language can only be provided through extensive reading and listening. The transfer of linguistic knowledge from receptive to productive repertoires is probably a relatively slow process, but it does take place, as the study of language acquisition shows. There are good linguistic reasons why in teaching we should do our utmost to take advantage of the wider exposure that reading and listening activities offer.

The nature of linguistic meaning is such that the acquisition of meaning is a continuing process. Since it is the product of highly complex networks of relationships between linguistic items, it can be learned only if the language is experienced sufficiently for those networks to be built up in the learner. The networks of associations developed in coursebooks and in readers which are structurally and lexically tied to the accompanying textbooks fall far short of those that the native speaker is aware of. This is, of course, a target that no foreign-language learner can hope to reach, but an adequate knowledge of semantic systems even for the language learner requires a good deal more than the textbook usually provides. The planned content of the textbook cannot give him a knowledge of collocational restrictions in the language either. This is something that is better learned through wide exposure.

Syntactic knowledge cannot be built up fully through step-by-step productive procedures. In the usual approach individual linguistic structures are progressively accumulated. Without there being any need to question this approach at this point, since the number of actual sentence structures in a language is potentially infinite, they could not all be enumerated in any course and could not be acquired by a simple additive process. The structural content of the first years of language courses certainly does not include all the possible structures in the language. Learners must have the opportunity to learn those aspects of syntactic structure which are not explicitly taught. If their syntactic experience is limited to what the course-book provides, there will be a severe limitation in their capacity to exploit the grammatical system of the language. By being exposed through reading and listening to language whose linguistic content is not kept wholly within what the productive syllabus contains, they can gradually build up this wider syntactic knowledge. Given that learners do possess some capacity for recognising in other people's language performance linguistic information that is relevant to their own learning of the language, reading and listening are a useful source of feedback for the learner. They provide him with continuing information about the grammatical systems with which he is already partly familiar.

D Wilkins
Second-language learning and teaching (Arnold 1974) pp 66–68

1   a   What is meant by the term 'receptive skills'?
    b   Do you agree that it is wrong to think of them as passive? Give your reasons.

2   The author expresses two reservations about the role given to productive language activities.
    a   What are these reservations and why does he hold that they inhibit language learning? Do you agree with him?
    b   Are there any special considerations that make it desirable or necessary for us to pay particular attention to the teaching of oral production in the classroom?

3   The author argues that we should 'take advantage of the wider exposure that reading and listening activities offer'.
    a   Examine any recent coursebooks at both the elementary and post-elementary level to see whether comprehension is allowed to develop ahead of production.
    b   What steps could be taken to supplement a course which does not make sufficient provision for language exposure through listening and reading?

FOR FURTHER REFERENCE

1   J P B Allen and H G Widdowson in J P B Allen and S Pit Corder (Eds)   *The Edinburgh Course in Applied Linguistics Volume 3* (OUP 1974) *Reading and Writing.*
2   D Byrne   *Teaching Oral English* (Longman 1976) Chapter 2.

4.3 Listening

Listening is in many ways more exacting than reading. The reader can stop, look up a word, reflect; he can slow down when the information is dense or the exposition difficult; he can even re-read complex passages. The listener, of course, has no such advantages. 5 'Neologophobia' – the fear of new words – is then, often more acute in listening than in reading. Panic, which attends the first unknown word in a discourse, may become paralysis after the second or third. Even some of the most able students underestimate – because of limited experience – the difficulties in continuous listening. Often 10 they lack the learning strategies and the positive psychological attitudes which alone can sustain them.

But listening makes special demands on the grammatical as well as the lexical skills of the listener. The foreign learner, because English is not his native language and is therefore not handled 15 automatically, is less able to predict the pattern of a sentence through its initial grammatical signals. Thus, when a native speaker of English hears the word 'neither' (plus an article) he automatically knows that it will be followed in a later part of the sentence by 'nor'; similarly 'not only' will be followed by 'but also'; and 'the more' 20 + adverb (in sentence initial position) will be repeated by the same structure in a subsequent clause. Until the student attains native-speaker control over these patterns – a very different thing from merely 'knowing' them – he will tend to understand as he hears, rather as the young English primary-school child reads as he sees, 25 not yet having the facility to force his mind ahead of the voices. The result is that he is less able to hold a continuous argument in his head, so fully occupied is he in decoding the on-going speech.

This necessary ability – to hold a line of thought in his head whilst listening – may also be impaired by the difficulty he finds with 30 cohesives and discourse markers: those items which bind sentences together and indicate the structure of the discourse. Perhaps because linguistics has not yet learned how to handle discourse effectively, very little attention has been devoted to what may prove a crucial area in aural comprehension. Pronominal usage, whether simple – 'it, 35 them, those' – or more complex – 'the former, the latter, the second factor we mentioned earlier' – seems to cause some difficulty for students. The exact meaning of some inter- and intra-sentence connectives frequently eludes the student: one thinks straightaway of such items as 'however', 'whilst', and 'since', with their unfortunate potential for ambiguity. Sometimes, too, the student is not conversant with some of the spoken markers of importance such as:

'What I'm really trying to get at here is . . .'
'The point at issue is . . .'
'This is really the nub . . .'

and so while trying to decode the signalling devices he misses what has been signalled.

To listen effectively, however, is not just a question of recognition and passive absorption. The listener should be mentally checking, supporting, challenging, and extrapolating the items of information contained in the discourse. He may often feel it necessary to write notes. Note-taking is a complex, demanding skill even in his first language. Aural analysis such as this rarely receives systematic or thorough training in classroom teaching. This training is urgently required.

K James & L Mullen
English as she is heard (in English Language Teaching Journal XXVIII.1 1973) pp 21–22

1 Explain in your own words why listening may be regarded as more 'exacting' than reading.

2 The authors refer to the 'special difficulties' which are made on the listener at the *grammatical* (i.e. sentence) level and at the *discourse* (i.e. above the sentence) level.
What examples do they give of these difficulties? Can you give other examples of your own?

3 Suggest steps which could be taken in the classroom to *prepare* students for listening difficulties. To what extent do you think it would help to support these through a sound training in *reading* skills?

FOR FURTHER REFERENCE

1 N Coe *Comprehension inside and outside the classroom* (Modern English Teacher 6.1 1978).
2 R V White *Listening Comprehension and Note-taking* (Modern English Teacher 6.1 and 6.2 1978).

3 K Chastain *The Development of Modern Language Skills* (Rand McNally 1971) Chapter 7.
4 G Brown *Listening to Spoken English* (Longman 1977).

4.4   The Listening Skill

Listening to a foreign language may be analysed as involving two levels of activity, both of which must be taught. The first, the recognition level, involves the identification of words and phrases in their structural interrelationships, of time sequences, logical and
5 modifying terms, and of phrases which are redundant interpolations adding nothing to the development of the line of thought. The second is the level of selection, where the listener is drawing out from the communication those elements which seem to him to contain the gist of the message. This process requires him to concentrate his
10 attention on certain sound groupings while others are aurally perceived without being retained. This parallels the process in visual perception where we see the object which attracts our attention but do not absorb surrounding details, which, from the physical point of view, are equally within the range of our view. For the student to be
15 able to listen with ease to the foreign language in normal situations, he needs thorough training at the recognition level and much practice in selecting specific details from the stream of sound.

   Training at the recognition level must begin from the first lesson. This does not mean the presentation of much ungraded and ill-
20 designed aural material in the hope that something will happen. There was a period when teachers were urged to surround their students from the very beginning with a veritable mist of foreign-language speech, thus recreating in the classroom, so it was believed, the situation in which students would find themselves if suddenly
25 transported to the country where the language is spoken. It is true that, when plunged completely into the foreign-language atmos-phere, people do learn to interpret the sounds they are hearing, but to varying degrees of accuracy. One fact which is conveniently overlooked is that many migrants in a new land are unable, after
30 many years of residence, to interpret more than the simple interchanges of daily life. Some do go beyond the comprehension of banalities but certainly not without effort on their part. When we take into consideration the number of hours during which the average migrant listens to the new language before he understands it
35 to any degree of effectiveness we appear justified in assuming that he is not learning aural comprehension in the most economical and

efficient way. In the considerably fewer hours at the disposal of the
teacher in the classroom, methods must be adopted which will lead
more directly to the objective, developing the greatest degree of skill
40 that is possible in the time available.

For a method to be economical as well as efficient it must take into
account all the skill elements which should be developed. As we have
seen, in a listening situation the student must be so familiar with the
components of a stream of speech that he can react quickly to some
45 of them and pass rapidly over others which are redundant or
irrelevant to his immediate purpose. He must be able to recognise
without effort sound patterns (sound discriminations affecting
meaning, intonation patterns, significant levels of pitch, word
groupings), grammatical sequences and tenses, modifiers and func-
50 tion words, clichés, expletives or hesitation expressions which can be
ignored as irrelevant to the message, levels of discourse (colloquial
or formal), emotional overtones (excited, disappointed, peremp-
tory, cautious, angry, utterances), as well as regional, social or
dialectal variations. As these aspects of speech become familiar to
55 the student his expectation of their occurrence in certain contexts
rises and their information content is, as a consequence, lessened. As
the human organism is able to absorb only a certain amount of
information at one time, this familiarity, by decreasing the information content, increases the number of items with which the student
60 can cope in one utterance. Systematically prepared listening comprehension materials will provide training, in a steady progression,
for all the areas listed, not leaving essential learning to chance. If
suitable materials are not available, the teacher will choose, adapt
and re-fashion those which are obtainable, or prepare his own, with
65 these basic requirements in mind.

W Rivers
Listening Comprehension in K Croft (Ed) *Readings on English as a
Second Language* (Winthrop 1980) pp 270–271

1 The author says that listening to a foreign language involves two
levels of activity.
a What are these levels and what does each involve?
b Why does she stress that both must be *taught*?

2 a What does the author mean by 'systematically prepared'
listening comprehension materials?
b Why does she reject the use of ungraded materials? In your

opinion, is there some use for ungraded materials for listening comprehension practice, even at a fairly early level of language training? Give your reasons.

3 Examine any coursebook to see what provision is made for developing listening comprehension skills. Decide whether the training they provide is systematic.

FOR FURTHER REFERENCE

1 G Broughton et al. *Teaching English as a Foreign Language* (Routledge and Kegan Paul 1978) pp 66–76.
2 R C Sittler *Teaching Aural Comprehension* (English Teaching Forum Special Issue: The Art of TESOL Part 1 1975).
3 A Maley *The Teaching of Listening Comprehension Skills* (Modern English Teacher 6.3 1978).

4.5 Extensive Listening

The teaching purpose of extensive listening practice is to give the learner plenty of opportunity to develop and exercise his listening skills in as natural a way as possible. Extensive listening need not be tested in any detail, but will be done for its own sake. The pupil will
5 be following the meaning of the listening passage, because he is interested in the information in it, or simply because he is enjoying it.

What would extensive listening materials look like? Obviously this depends on the level of learner that they are intended for, but it is very important that they should be varied. Recordings of stories and
10 other texts taken from books or magazines can often be used. But for the more advanced learners, it is rather important to get away from language that has been specially controlled for teaching purposes and that was also written rather than spoken in the first place. Recordings from the radio and television are the obvious
15 sources of spontaneous conversation. Listening materials to give practice in making sense of unscripted language can also be specially made if enough native speakers are available to make recordings. Variety does not only mean different topics, it also means different kinds of language, different accents and dialects, different styles of
20 talking and so on.

Should the language content of these passages be controlled? Again the answer depends on how advanced in their study of the foreign language the pupils are. Listening texts for beginners are unlikely to be found in sources originally meant for native speakers.
25 They would be too difficult, so special passages would probably have to be constructed for this level. As a course progresses into the more advanced stages, however, the distinction between language for learners and language for native-speakers becomes less and less marked until eventually for all practical purposes it can be
30 disregarded. It is important that extensive listening materials should not slavishly follow the set syllabus of a teaching course – that would defeat the purpose of the exercise. There should be not only familiar words and phrases in new contexts, but also new words and phrases which the pupil has to try to make sense of.

35 How many new items? In the end the answer depends on the reaction the teacher gets from the pupils. If they fail to follow a

passage, it may mean that there are too many new words. But it may not. It may mean only that they have missed one or two of the 'key items' in the text. We shall come back to key items in a moment.

How should extensive listening practice be prepared for? We have suggested that it should be done for its own sake, but this need not mean that the teacher would take no interest in it at all. Ideally, a period of extensive listening, particularly in lower-level classes, would be introduced by familiarising the pupils with the general context of the listening passage, perhaps by looking at a photograph or a picture with them, asking one or two questions about it and perhaps even making sure that they know the meaning of some of the key items which can be seen in the picture or defined verbally. The purpose of this introductory work, which will not of course take long nor go into great detail, is to put the pupils in the right frame of mind for the listening practice, and in this way make it much easier for them to make sense of the language in the passage.

The term 'key items' is not synonymous with 'useful words in English'. They are items which in a particular passage play a specifically significant role in the structure of the passage, so that a failure to understand them is very likely to lead to a failure to understand a large section of the passage, if not all of it. Either these items must be known before the pupils do the practice, or they must be made very clear from the context, perhaps with the use of sound effects in the recording or the histrionic abilities of the speakers.

A Howatt & J Dakin
Language Laboratory Materials in J P B Allen and S Pit Corder (Eds) *The Edinburgh Course in Applied Linguistics* Volume 3 (OUP 1974) pp 94–95

1 From your reading of this passage how would you define the term 'extensive listening'?

2 The authors ask four questions:
  (i) What would extensive listening materials look like?
  (ii) Should the language content of these passages be controlled?
  (iii) How many new items (should they contain)?
  (iv) How should extensive listening practice be prepared for?
  Say briefly what advice the authors offer in connection with each of these. Do you agree with it? Give your reasons.

3 Select a text, such as a story, which could be used for extensive

listening practice at an elementary level. (You may relate this to a specific course.) Identify what you think are the *key items* and say how you would *prepare* the class for listening to the text.

FOR FURTHER REFERENCE

1 J McAlpin *Using Recorded Dialogues in Class* (Modern English Teacher 5.3 and 5.4 1977).
2 A Maley *The Teaching of Listening Comprehension Skills* (Modern English Teacher 6.3 1978).
3 *ELT Materials: Design and Use No 5: The Listening Library* (British Council 1978).

4.6 Two Levels of Language Behaviour

If we can identify two levels of foreign-language behaviour for which our students must be trained, then it is clear that one type of teaching will not be sufficient for the task. These two levels may be designated: (1) the level of *manipulation* of language elements that
5 occur in fixed relationships in clearly defined systems (that is, relationships that will vary within very narrow limits), and (2) a level of *expression of personal meaning* at which possible variations are infinite, depending on such factors as the type of message to be communicated, the situation in which the utterance takes place, the
10 relationship between speaker and hearer or hearers, and the degree of intensity with which the message is conveyed. If we recognise two such levels, a place must be found for the firm establishment of certain basic linguistic habits and the understanding of a complex system with its infinite possibilities of expression. The problem is to
15 define the role of each of these types of learning and their inter-relationships in the acquiring of a foreign language.

It is essential to recognise first that certain elements of language remain in fixed relationships in small, closed systems, so that once the system is invoked in a particular way a succession of inter-related
20 formal features appears. Fluent speakers are able to make these inter-related adjustments irrespective of the particular message they wish to produce. The elements that interact in restricted systems may be practised intensively in order to forge strong habitual associations from which the speaker never deviates (this applies to
25 such elements as inflection of person and number, agreements of gender, fixed forms for interrogation or negation, formal features of tenses). These elements do not require intellectual analysis: they exist, and they must be used in a certain way in certain environments and in no other way. For these features, intensive practice exercises
30 of various kinds can be very effective learning procedures, with the teacher supplying a brief word of explanation where necessary to forestall hesitation or bewilderment. (Lengthy explanations can be a hindrance rather than a help for this type of activity because it is *how* these systems operate that matters, not *why*.)
35 At the second level, decisions more intimately connected with contextual meaning may bring into play any of a variety of syntactic

111

structures, so that students will be continually re-using what they have learned. A decision at this higher level has structural implications beyond the word or the phrase, often beyond the sentence. A
40 slight variation in the decision will often mean the construction of quite a different form of utterance. Naturally, then, decisions at the second level involve a more complicated initial choice, which entails further choices of a more limited character. In order to express exactly what one wishes to say, one must view it in relation to the
45 potential of the structural system of the language as a whole and select accordingly. This is the higher level decision that sets in motion operations at lower levels that are interdependent. The decision to make a particular type of statement about something that has taken place recently involves a choice of register, a choice of
50 degree of intensity, the use of lexical items in certain syntactical relationships that will involve the production of certain morphological elements, certain phonemic distinctions and certain stress and intonation patterns. The inter-relationships within the language system that are involved in these higher-level decisions often need to
55 be clarified in deductive fashion by the teacher or textbook. For effective practice at this level the student must understand the implications and ramifications of changes he is making. This he will do best if the practice involves making decisions in real communication situations devised in the classroom, rather than in artificial
60 drills and exercises. In such interchanges the feedback from the other participants in communication brings a realisation of the effect of the decisions the speaker has made.

There must be in the classroom, then, a constant interplay of learning by analogy and by analysis, of inductive and deductive
65 processes – according to the nature of the operation the student is learning. It is evident that he cannot put higher level choices into operation with ease if he has not developed facility in the production of the inter-dependent lower-level elements, and so learning by intensive practice and analogy have their place. Genuine freedom in
70 language use, however, will develop only as the student gains control of the system as a whole, beyond the mastery of patterns in isolation. This control will become established only through much experience in attempting to counterbalance and inter-relate various syntactic possibilities in order to convey a comprehensible meaning
75 in a situation where its expression has some real significance.

It would be a mistake, however, to believe that practice at the second level should be delayed until the student has learned all the common features of the manipulative type – that is, that the student should first learn to manipulate elements in fixed relationships and

not begin until a year or two later to learn the selection process of the
higher level. If he is eventually to understand a complex system with
its infinite possibilities of expression, he must develop this understanding little by little. The student will learn to make higher-level
selective decisions by being made aware at every step of the
5 meaningful use in communication of operations he is learning at the
manipulative level. No matter how simple the pattern he is
practising, he will become aware of its possibilities for communication when he attempts to use it for his own purposes and not just
to complete an exercise or to perform well in a drill.
10 Whether at the first or second level, practice does not have to be
boring or meaningless. It can take the form of games and
competitions which call for the production of the types of structures
being learned or conversational interchanges within a directional
framework. With a little thought, the classroom teacher can find
15 interesting, even exciting ways to practise all kinds of structural
combinations and inter-relationships until the student acquires
confidence and assurance in their potentialities of expression.

W Rivers
Speaking in Many Tongues (Newbury House 1972) pp 13–17
abridged

1 a What are the 'two levels of foreign-language behaviour'
       which the author identifies? Give examples of each.
   b What, according to the author, are their implications for
       teaching? Do you agree with her point of view?

2 Give your own opinion of the following:
   a Lengthy explanations can be a hindrance rather than a help
       (lines 32–33).
   b It would be a mistake to believe that practice at the second
       level should be delayed until the student has learned all the
       common features of the manipulative type (lines 76–78).

3 Suggest some activities at the manipulative level which would
   ensure that practice is not 'boring or meaningless'.

4 Examine any set of course materials at both the beginning and
   post-elementary levels to see what provision is made for teaching
   the author's two levels of language behaviour.

FOR FURTHER REFERENCE

1 W Rivers and M S Temperley *A Practical Guide to the Teaching of English* (OUP 1978) *Structured Interaction.*

2 C H Prator *The Development of a Manipulation-Communication Scale* (English Teaching Forum Special Issue: The Art of TESOL Part 1 1975).

3 C B Paulston in K Croft (Ed) *Readings on English as a Second Language* (Winthrop 1980) *The Sequencing of Structural Pattern Drills.*

4.7 The Language of Dialogues

In setting up dialogues, the writer (or the teacher) should always keep the 'social dimension' in mind – that is, who is speaking to whom and the 'social status' of each speaker. Otherwise the students will have no possibility of learning the important distinctions
5 between formal and informal speech. For example:

>   (*Teacher to student*)
>   Teacher: Good morning.
>   Student: Good morning.
>   Teacher: How are you today?
0 >   Student: Fine, thank you.
>
>   (*Student to another student he knows well*)
>   Student 1: Hi.
>   Student 2: Hi.
>   Student 1: How're you doing?
5 >   Student 2: Pretty good. How about you?
>   Student 1: Not bad.

The writer (or the teacher) should also keep the social dimension in mind when determining when and to whom one can safely ask such questions as *How old are you?* and *How much money do you make?*
20   There should be a variety of 'language samples'. While consistency in format is admirable, the fact remains that some structures occur naturally and frequently in conversation (*Me, too. I don't, do you?*) and others are more likely to occur in exposition, narration, and description (*After a long discussion, it was determined that many of the
25 old buildings, which were beyond repair, should be torn down to make way for new constructions*). Some textbook writers appear to assume that any language can be suitably presented in dialogue form. This simply is not the case.
    The language sample should be short enough for the student to
30 remember it easily but long enough to provide sufficient practice on the new structure. It is not always easy to decide about length, for there can never be an exact definition of what is too long and what is too short. Many students find memorising dialogues of ten or more exchanges difficult and boring, and they lose interest in the rest of the

35 lesson. On the other hand, a dialogue that has only one exchange will not contain enough material for drills and exercises. One technique for avoiding excessively long dialogues and prose passages is to break down the dialogue or reading into smaller, self-contained units that can be used as the basis for one or two drills. In this way
40 the students can concentrate on the new language items and are not needlessly slowed up or confused because they can't remember the details (the vocabulary or the situation) introduced in the language sample.

In devising contexts, the writer (or the teacher) should be careful
45 to include sentences that can be used for vocabulary development and communication activities – sentences that can be used as the basis for what Stevick calls a 'Cummings device'. For example, the following question-and-answer might occur in a dialogue:

S 1: Where did you go last night?
50   S 2: To a movie.

Such questions-and-answers can readily lend themselves to encouraging realistic conversation by providing alternate answers:

To a movie, a game, a concert.
I didn't go anywhere. I stayed at home.

55 Amazingly enough, many of us have ignored the need for alternate responses in realistic language practice. If a student is supposed to give a 'real' answer to a question such as *Where did you go last night?* he ought to have the option of answering that he didn't go anywhere.

Let me conclude with a brief mention of a promising new direction
60 contextualisation might take – a direction that, as far as I know, has received very little attention in the textbooks currently available. Simply stated, it takes into account what John Carroll has called the 'conditions of elicitation'. That is, it is concerned with the circumstances or conditions under which a speaker will produce a certain kind
65 of sentence.

The need to consider 'conditions of elicitation' was forcefully brought home to me by a story I heard recently. Most ESL texts require the students very early to practise the identification pattern *This is a (book)*. Yet few of us have wondered just when and how
70 often we actually use such a statement. Recently, it seems, an experienced ESL teacher found himself using this sentence and was so amazed that he immediately made note of it. The teacher had gone to the post office to mail a book that was carefully wrapped in brown paper. When he went to the window, he said to the clerk, 'This is a
75 book.' When he recovered from the shock of realising what he had

said, he began to ask himself why he had said it. The reason is clear enough. As Carroll has postulated, 'Declarative sentences are normally uttered when the speaker perceives his own information as greater than that of his hearers.' Since the man behind the counter did not know what was in the package, he had to be told. The story
5 has an obvious moral: should we ask our students to 'make statements' simply in order to practise their form, or should we ask them to make statements in a context where a statement is naturally called for?

What I am suggesting is that the ideal context might well go
10 beyond the situation itself to specify the conditions under which the sentences in the language sample are suitable. Granted, such precise specification would be difficult, and it might not be possible to achieve in every lesson. Still, the approach is worth trying. It certainly seems more reasonable to ask a question because you don't
15 know the answer than to ask one in order to practise question forms.

W R Slager

Creating Contexts for Language Practice (in TESOL Quarterly 7.1 1973) pp 2–4

1 *'Some textbook writers appear to assume that any language can be suitably presented in dialogue form'* (lines 26–28).

   a What recommendations does the author make about the language of dialogues?
   b Are the criticisms he makes generally true of dialogues in recently published textbooks?

2 What is *your* answer to the question: 'Should we ask our students to 'make statements' simply in order to practise their form, or should we ask them to make statements in a context where a statement is naturally called for?' Are both types of practice justifiable in certain circumstances? Give your reasons.

3 On the basis of this extract, make a list of criteria which could be used for the evaluation of textbook dialogues. Add any other ideas of your own.

   Use the list you have compiled to evaluate sample dialogues in any commonly used coursebook.

FOR FURTHER REFERENCE

1 J Dobson *Dialogues: Why, When and How to Teach them* (English Teaching Forum Special Issue: The Art of TESOL Part 1 1975).

2   D Byrne   *Teaching Oral English* (Longman 1976) Chapter 4.
3   D Girard   *Linguistics and Foreign Language Teaching* (Longman 1972) Chapter 3.
4   I E Stanislawsczyk and S Yavena   *Creativity in the Language Classroom* (Newbury House 1969).

4.8 Communication Practice

The most effective communication practice is that which is built up around the people, places, and things with which the students are familiar. As far as possible, it should take into account their age level, individual interests, hobbies, the work they do or the other subjects they study, the locality in which they live, and as many other details relevant to their daily lives as possible. This, of course, requires the teacher to spend a fair amount of time getting to know the students personally, so that he may guide the practice into those areas in which they would be most eager to express themselves in real-life communication. It also requires each student to familiarise himself with his classmates' backgrounds and interests in those cases where there is little opportunity for social contact outside of the classroom.

There is no doubt that all this puts a considerable burden on a teacher with a large number of classes. But if the work is systematised (with the aid of notes in the class records, for example) the problem can certainly be solved. Even the knowledge of rather trivial facts about individual students can be used to great advantage in communication practice. If it is known, for example, that Mr Ito, a company employee, is keen on mahjong, or that Miss Sato, a tennis player, is planning to attend her club's summer training camp, these facts can be used over and over again for practice on a great variety of structures.

Humour, and even a certain amount of teasing (provided there is no unpleasantness and the students involved can take it), should also be encouraged, as it contributes greatly to a relaxed atmosphere well suited to the give-and-take of natural conversation. This can sometimes be achieved by having a student imagine himself in some extraordinary or ridiculous situation, which forms the basis for the communication practice. Even though such a situation may be far removed from ordinary life, it is worthwhile making an exception here to the general rule of creating 'real life' situations, because the very fact of it being so incongruous means that the patterns associated with the situation are more likely to be remembered.

Classroom objects are convenient and familiar things to talk about, and they certainly have a part to play in habituation and

communication at elementary levels. However, they cannot by any
stretch of the imagination be called interesting objects. Also, since
their usefulness is confined to the classroom, and since the purpose
40 of the communication practice is precisely to escape from the
classroom setting, it is not advisable to dwell too long on such items
as blackboards, erasers, red pencils, blue notebooks, my textbook,
your pencil box, and other classroom paraphernalia, which people
simply do not talk about in real life.
45　　It is also important to make the situations as concrete as possible.
Persons, places, and things should be named rather than referred to
as generic concepts. Rather than saying that he went to the movies
with 'my friend' (which, by the way, should usually be corrected to
'one of my friends' or 'a friend of mine') a student should be
50 encouraged to say 'with Noriko', 'with Tanaka kun', etc. Instead of
buying something in 'the department store' he should buy it in
Daimaru or Takashimaya (or any other local name). For specific
articles, brand names should be used. The textbook naturally has to
refer to things in a more general way, but in real life people usually
55 talk about specific persons, places, and things, and this fact should
be reflected in the communication practice. Being specific also
enables the members of the class to share with each other in building
up a whole list of familiar characters and definite places and things –
all of which adds greater reality to the practice.

D P Cosgrave
From Pattern Practice to Communication (in English Teaching
Forum Special Issue: The Art of TESOL Part 1 1975)

1　The author argues that 'the most effective communication
practice is that which is built up around the people, places and
things with which the students are familiar' (lines 1–3).
a　Do you agree with this? Give your reasons.
b　Can you think of other effective ways of devising communication practice?

2　Are all students likely to be equally willing to talk about
themselves? What are some of the problems involved in this
approach?

3　Examine two or three units from any coursebook for the early
stages of language learning to see what opportunities there
would be for making 'the situations as concrete as possible' (line
45).

FOR FURTHER REFERENCE

1 P Cole *Some Techniques for Communication Practice* (English Teaching Forum Special Issue: The Art of TESOL Part 1 1975).

2 W Rivers *Speaking in Many Tongues* (Newbury House 1972) *Talking Off the Tops of their Heads.*

3 D Byrne *Teaching Oral English* (Longman 1976) Chapter 8.

4 A Lipson in R Lugton (Ed) *Towards a Cognitive Approach to Second Language Behaviour* (Center for Curriculum Development 1971) *Some New Strategies for Teaching Oral Skills.*

5 SJ Savignon *Communicative Competence: An Experiment in Foreign-Language Teaching* (Center for Curriculum Development 1972).

4.9 The Reading Skill

Before considering efficient approaches to the teaching of reading, it is essential to distinguish clearly two activities which go by this name, but which must not for that reason be confused with each other. A student may be considered to be 'reading' when he stands
5 up in class and enunciates in the conventional way the sounds which are symbolised by the printed or written marks on the script in his hand. This he may do in a way which is acceptable and comprehensible to a native speaker, without drawing meaning from what he is reading. This activity is one aspect of reading for which
10 the student must be trained, but it is not the final goal in the foreign-language classroom. He must also be taught to derive meaning from the word combinations in the text and to do this in a consecutive fashion at a reasonable speed, without necessarily vocalising what he is reading. He has learned to do this in his own language, but he is
15 now faced with a different language code and one with which he is far from familiar.

In reading, then, the student is 'developing a considerable range of habitual responses to a specific set of patterns of graphic shapes'. When learning to read his native language he has acquired essential
20 space and direction habits: he can recognise the shapes of letters in his native-language alphabet and he has become skilled at reading these in the direction his language prescribes. He has also learned to recognise certain patterns of arrangement (such as paragraph divisions) and is familiar with the punctuation marks and their
25 function. When he comes to read in the foreign language, then, he already understands what the process of reading signifies. He is alert to the fact that reading involves recognition of certain patterns of symbols and that these represent particular sounds which form words he may use, or may hear spoken. He has also
30 come to recognise with ease particular words which clarify the function of other words close to them, and words which indicate logical relationships among segments of sentences or sections of discourse. He has also been trained in rapid identification of word groups which have a meaning transcending the meaning of the
35 individual units of which they are composed. This means that he has learned to extract from the printed patterns three levels of meaning:

lexical meaning (the semantic content of the words and expressions), structural and grammatical meaning (deriving from inter-relationships among words, or parts of words, or from the order of words), and socio-cultural meaning (the evaluation which people of his own culture attach to the words or groups of words he is reading).

If the foreign language employs the same alphabet as the student's native language and is a cognate language (as is the case with English and French, or English and German), his well-practised reading habits may hinder him considerably in extracting from the foreign-language text these three levels of meaning. He will see familiar combinations of letters which signal distinctively different sounds. He will recognise some combinations of letters, identical with those of his native language, which signal different lexical or socio-cultural meanings. He will, at times, encounter a word order which has a different structural or grammatical meaning from that which his native language has taught him to expect.

The foreign-language teacher often assumes that because his students have already acquired reading skill in their native language, reading in the foreign language should not be difficult for them. It should now be clear that the main element transferred from the student's training in native-language reading is a certain comprehension of what reading is about and a certain awareness of the importance of letter and word combinations. Very little else is of great help to him. Unlike the child learning to read his native language, the student is not recognising symbols for words and expressions with which he already has considerable acquaintance. If he is forced to read in the foreign language too early in the course, he finds himself adrift in a flood of words and expressions he has never before encountered; with a similar alphabet he is impeded by interference from well-established native-language habits; structural clues are all awry. Forced to decipher with the aid of a dictionary, he transfers native-language pronunciations to the foreign-language text, attaches inaccurate lexical meanings to units, and is misled in interpretation by his previous cultural experience.

Some teachers will argue that plenty of experience with a considerable quantity of reading material is essential from an early stage of language learning, in order to expand the student's knowledge of the language. This will give him, they maintain, experience with a much wider range of expressions and structures than he could gain from listening and speaking, which are limited to his time in laboratory or classroom. Let us examine, at this point, one of the practices commonly observed in foreign-language classes

80 where the students spend much of their time reading. We may
question whether real knowledge of the language, beyond casual
acquaintance with some isolated elements of it, is attained by the
following procedure which is common among students: the student
deciphers a part of the text with the help of a bilingual dictionary or
85 word list; he hurriedly writes a native-language near-equivalent
above each unfamiliar word in the text and rushes on to find out
further trivial details of a banal story (as often as not artificially
constructed to include certain grammatical forms). If the student
does pause to reread, he skips through a hotch-potch of text, with his
90 eye leaping from foreign words to interlinear native-language
glosses. This is certainly not reading in the second sense of the term.
It is doubtful whether it is even an educative experience which can be
defended in the face of pressures on school time.

W Rivers
Teaching Foreign-language Skills (University of Chicago Press 1968)
pp 215–217

1 The author refers to two activities which are commonly called
'reading'.

a What are they and what does each involve?

b In your view, which of these is best regarded as truly
'reading'? Give your reasons.

2 a Mention some of the advantages and disadvantages of asking
students to read aloud.

b What steps would you take to ensure that students read
aloud in an acceptable fashion?

3 *When he comes to read in the foreign language the student already*
'understands what the process of reading signifies' (lines 25–26).

How does the author describe the process of reading? Do you
agree with her description? Give your reasons.

4 Why does the author take a cautious view of allowing students to
read early on in the foreign language course? Do you agree with
her point of view or would you allow a wide exposure to the
foreign language through reading?

FOR FURTHER REFERENCE

1 W Norris *Advanced Reading: Goals, Techniques and Procedures*
(English Teaching Forum Special Issue: The Art of TESOL Part 2
1975).

2   A Davies and H G Widdowson in J P B Allen and S Pit Corder (Eds)   *The Edinburgh Course in Applied Linguistics* Volume 3 (OUP 1975) *Reading and Writing.*

3   H G Widdowson   *Explorations in Applied Linguistics* (OUP 1979) *The Process and Purpose of Reading.*

4   P Strevens   *New Orientations in the Teaching of English* (OUP 1977) Chapter 9.

5   F Smith   *Reading* (CUP 1978).

4.10   In Defence of Writing

It is often taken for granted that speaking a foreign language is more important than writing it. The natural and seemingly logical consequence of this is that, on the standard language-course, the top priority is given to speaking activities. Writing, if it appears at all, is
5 given only a small place in the general plan. What I would like to suggest is that (a) writing is important and (b) paradoxically, we can only improve our spoken language by writing.

The importance of writing is coming to be more and more recognised. It is through the written mode that links with the outside
10 world are formed. Whereas we need a listener in order to speak, a reader can be found anywhere within reach of a postman. And books and magazines are even handier than records, tapes, and radio broadcasts. But writing has a further advantage: it can help us to speak.
15 The sad fact is that many people, when asked how well they can speak a foreign language, think immediately of pronunciation. But this is only one aspect of speaking and a relatively unimportant one at that. Only prospective teachers, who have to act as substitutes for native speakers, i.e. as models, need to concentrate on really good
20 pronunciation. Apart from them, and a few others in special jobs, most learners need only progress to a point where they can make the important distinctions and produce stress and intonation patterns which do not confuse or upset the listener. Only the talented few ever achieve a near-native accent. More important than pronunciation
25 are vocabulary and structures. These aspects are, by and large, common to both speaking and writing. Furthermore, a mastery of them is within the grasp of most learners who are willing to concentrate enough.

Given the fact that the vital and most attainable goals of language
30 learning are certain aspects of both the written and the spoken mode of language communication, it remains to decide which is the most helpful in learning or whether both are equally valuable. The great disadvantage of the speaking situation, in a natural language interchange, is that much information that passes from speaker to
35 listener and vice versa can be gained from the general context and from expressions of the body and face. As everybody knows, it is

126

much easier to survive in a speaking situation without resorting to one's knowledge of vocabulary and structure. A relatively poor grasp of the language can be amazingly effective in achieving and maintaining a certain basic level of communication. Not only can one guess a great deal from the context, one can also keep quiet when one is unable to say anything and, by means of hesitations, get the listener to supply missing items (often without his knowledge!). There are, for example, a whole list of fillers in English, like er, um, you know what I mean, well I mean, actually, really, and all that, and the much beloved but almost archaic (or at least overused) and whatnot. One is restricted to situations where such expressions are adequate to keep the conversation going. A mastery of such linguistic (or socio-linguistic) techniques to bolster up a fairly weak knowledge of the language often provokes initial admiration on the part of native speakers: 'How well you speak English', 'You are almost a native speaker!' and so on. It only takes one demand for special information, or one unusual utterance, to reveal the gaps in one's mastery of the language. An overreliance on these techniques and on the presence of a sufficiently sensitive and sympathetic listener may bring quick success of a superficial kind but one which vanishes with the first real obstacle. It is then the 'fluency' may be revealed in its true guise of 'glibness'.

An extreme example, but one which is familiar to most teachers, is the learner who can chatter away for hours in the target language without ever really saying anything. The worst aspect of this is that the learner is often firmly convinced that he need not study the language any further. Learning only to speak the target language may actually retard the learning process. It is only in a writing situation where so many of the external props are removed (no gestures, no listener, no objects in the room, etc.) that one is forced to concentrate on perfecting one's mastery of the language system to provide the adequate means for communicating something in the target language. It therefore becomes vital to increase the time devoted to teaching in the written mode. Only by writing can we ever hope to rise above the glib level and develop a proper command of the system which will show immediate results in both written and spoken performance. A stimulating approach to the teaching of modern written English should ensure success in speaking, and a success of a much less superficial kind than the success referred to above. Practice in writing may not help with the dental fricatives but, much more important, it will promote a sophisticated and flexible command of the language. Moreover, this more valuable type of success is within the range of many learners who will never be able to pronounce the dental fricatives!

M Sharwood Smith
A Note on 'Writing versus Speech' (in English Language Teaching
Journal XXXI.1 1976) pp 17–19

1 Give your views on the following:
   a Only prospective teachers need to concentrate on really good
     pronunciation.
   b Vocabulary and structure are more important than
     pronunciation.
   c Learning only to speak the target language may actually
     retard the learning process.

2 *'It is much easier to survive in a speaking situation without
   resorting to one's knowledge of vocabulary and structure'* (lines
   36–38).

   How does the author support this statement? Do you agree with
   him? Give your reasons.

3 In your opinion, does the author substantiate his assertion that
   'we can only improve our spoken language by writing'? What is
   your own point of view?

4 From your experience of teaching or learning a foreign language
   do you agree that more attention should be paid to the teaching
   of writing? Give your reasons if they are different from the
   author's.

FOR FURTHER REFERENCE

1 L Winer *Quiet: People Communicating* (Modern English
  Teacher 6.3 1978).

4.11 The Importance of Connectives in Writing

When students progress from writing sentences in exercises to putting sentences together in paragraphs, they must begin learning about a new set of relationships. As they have had to learn the relationships within the sentence, they must now learn the relationships between sentences.

Written sentences in combination involve a complex inter-twining of structural, lexical, semantic, and logical relationships. The more written discourse is examined from different points of view, the more aware one becomes of the various kinds of relationships that exist and of the fact that they are really inextricable from one another. The intention here, however, is merely to call attention to some of the basic connections that students need to learn about as soon as they begin to use sentences in sequence.

Since there is a good deal to be learned about sentence connections, students should begin writing paragraphs very early. It need not and should not be postponed until students reach an intermediate or advanced level, but should begin at a very elementary level, as soon as students are able to produce simple sentences. Much of what needs to be learned must come from the experience of writing, since many points are not covered in textbooks.

Sentences in written discourse must be linked together in some manner; if not, they fall apart completely. The links consist of a variety of devices, such as pronouns, demonstratives, articles, conjunctions, conjunctive adverbs, prepositional phrases, repetition of key words, parallel structure, and synonyms – to name which are perhaps the commonest. By means of this linkage the movement of ideas from sentence to sentence and from paragraph to paragraph is brought about.

These devices, varied though they are, actually represent 'a subtle repetition'. 'Every sentence in a composition must repeat, directly or indirectly, a particle of or the total idea of the preceding sentence. Repetition builds the bridges of transition over which ideas . . . pass in ordered columns'.

A student of composition must also become aware of the fact that a sentence can be complete as far as grammar is concerned, but dependent as far as its position in a sequence is concerned. A few sentences will illustrate:

> Their ideas about education have changed.
> But cotton takes chemicals from the soil.
40 Then the style changed and skirts became very short.
> A space suit also requires heavy shoes.
> Many are attractive but poorly built.

It will be seen that each of these sentences is dependent on preceding material and so can fit into a sequence only in a certain place. These 45 are only a few simple examples of the kind of dependency a student must become aware of as soon as he begins fitting sentences together. As his writing becomes more advanced, he will need to understand and use a greater variety of connectives.

These links can be classified in various ways. Some of them are 50 referential (Their ideas about education have changed), some are sequential (Then the style changed), some are additive (A space suit also requires heavy shoes), some are contrastive (But cotton takes chemicals from the soil), some are substitutional (Many are attractive but poorly built), etc.

55 Classification of connectives is complicated by the fact that many of them have both grammatical and logical functions. They not only serve as links between sentences (and parts of sentences), but they also indicate the logical nature of the connection; that is, they express such relationships as addition, causation, comparison, 60 contrast, result, summary etc. Certain types of connectives, particularly conjunctions and conjunctive adverbs, are more or less adequately treated in textbooks on composition, but, as already indicated, many types of sentence links are not.

V Horn
Using Connectives in Elementary Composition (in English Language
Teaching XXVI.2 (1972) pp 154–155

1 *'Sentences in written discourse must be linked together in some manner'* (lines 21–22).

  a What linking devices are mentioned by the author?

  b How many examples of these can you find in the first paragraph?

  c Why are these linking devices more important in writing than in speech?

2 a Explain what is meant by 'a sentence can be complete as far as

grammar is concerned but dependent as far as its position in a sequence (of sentences) is concerned'.

b Choose any two of the illustrative sentences given by the author and suggest what sentence or sentences may have preceded them.

3 a Do you agree with the author's recommendation that 'students should begin writing paragraphs very early'.

b Do most coursebooks make adequate provision for writing connected sentences at the elementary level? Suggest some ways of providing appropriate practice.

FOR FURTHER REFERENCE

1 A Pincas *Writing in Paragraphs* (English Language Teaching XXIV.2 1970).
2 A Tadros *A Look Beyond the Sentence* (English Teaching Forum XIV.2 1976).
3 D Byrne *Teaching Writing Skills* (Longman 1979) Chapter 2 and Appendix 1.

4.12 Integrating Reading and Writing

Integrating skills in the language programme is not a new idea, and most teachers today are aware of the benefits to be derived from using the four skills as a means of presenting, practising and extending one and the same set of language forms and functions.
5 Obviously there are limitations in adopting a totally integrated approach because there are important differences between the written and spoken forms of the language. An indiscriminate use of an integrated approach may obscure such differences with the result that pupils may write in a manner more appropriate to spoken
10 communication. The transfer of forms from one context to another is no problem, however, if the transfer occurs within the same medium, and it is for such facilitative transfer that I would like to give some suggestions.

When we write, we also read. Indeed, it is necessary to do so, since
15 the process of creating a piece of written discourse depends on reading over what has already been written in order to formulate the next step in the discourse preparatory to writing it down. Even before we write, we often read for information which is subsequently to be incorporated in our own composition. In addition, the form
20 and style of the composition itself will also be shaped by what we know of the status, tastes and characteristics of the reader. So, the process of writing depends upon reading before, during and after the act of creating, and the writer who takes no account of the fact that he is writing something for someone to read runs the risk of
25 producing a text that is unreadable.

Given the complementarity of reading and writing, it would seem sensible to capitalise on the integration of these two skills in teaching our pupils to write. There are a number of advantages to be derived from doing this. Firstly, the reading text can provide an example of
30 the type of text which the students themselves should produce. This doesn't mean that the text is simply there to be slavishly imitated. What it does mean is that the student has an example which is a piece of communication consisting of sentences that are grammatically connected and logically linked. Secondly, individual language forms
35 and functions are presented in context in a continuous piece of discourse. The pupil's attention can be drawn to the items concerned

132

and even though practice may necessitate decontextualised manipulation, the existence of a context in which the items belong helps to avoid the dangers inherent in such practice exercises. Furthermore, the full meaning of an item – structural or functional – is not revealed until it is seen in a context as provided by the reading text.

Thirdly, the reading text can be drawn from the type of language which the students themselves need to read and write. This is especially the case for students whose need to learn and use English falls within the institutional rather than the personal domain, a distinction which can be exemplified by the difference between writing a report (institutional) and writing a short story (personal). Fourthly, the reading text can provide the basis for reading comprehension exercises which focus on the way the text is structured and organised. An understanding of such organisation is, of course, a prerequisite for constructing a piece of coherent prose. Thus, the comprehension exercise can provide a valuable basis for subsequent written production of a parallel text.

Finally, the use of information transfer exercises when dealing with the reading text can provide the student with information to be written up in the next phase of the lesson using the completed table, diagram or illustration as a cue. The use of such a visual cue means that he is reconstructing the message (or part of the original) without, however, merely lifting chunks of language from the original text to produce a poorly assimilated copy. The act of reconstituting the information from, say, a visual form into a verbal form 'using your own words' is facilitated if the cue for writing is already one step removed from the original text.

R V White
Integrating Reading and Writing (in Modern English Teacher 6.3
1978)

1 What does the author mean by the assertion that the 'process of writing depends upon reading before, during and after the act of creation'?
2 a Why does the author have reservations about the adoption of a 'totally integrated approach'?
   b Can you suggest some tasks or activities where it would be appropriate to transfer from the spoken to the written medium?

3 The author mentions a number of advantages to be gained from integrating reading and writing.

a What are these advantages?

b Later in his article the author provides the following example of an activity to integrate reading and writing.

Exercise 1

The text opposite is a short narrative of a visit which Damien Sinclair made to Brazil last October.

a Read the text.

b (Ring) and number in sequence all the Base +ed verbs. There are 11 of them, and the first one is ringed and numbered for you.

c [Box] the place adverbials.

d Number the place adverbials in sequence.

e Use the information in the place adverbials to complete the table.

Text A Visit to Brazil

Last October, Damien Sinclair (arrived) [1] at Recife by air from England. After a few days in Recife, he travelled south to Salvador, where he stayed for a week. Then he continued south to Brasilia, which he reached after two days' travel. He spent two days in Brasilia, and then he went south to Belo Horizonte. Two days later, he moved further south to Rio de Janeiro, where he visited some friends. After a week of visiting and sightseeing in Rio, Damien drove to Sao Paolo. Finally, after several days there, he returned to London by plane.

FROM	TO	TIME THERE
England		a few days
	Belo Horizonte	
		Several days
		/////////////

Exercise 2

A list of places in sequence is called an ITINERARY. The table on page 134 is an itinerary of Damien Sinclair's journey through Brazil.

a   Use the itinerary in the table on page 134 to mark Damien's journey on the map.

b   Show the direction of his journey with arrows. The first stage of his journey is marked to show you what to do.

Show how it incorporates the advantages he mentions.

4   Devise an activity of your own which integrates reading and writing skills.

FOR FURTHER REFERENCE

1   S Moulding *Developing All Four Skills* (Modern English Teacher 5.4 1977).

2   C Kennedy *Exploiting a Text* (Modern English Teacher 6.3 1978).

3   D Byrne *Teaching Writing Skills* (Longman 1979) Chapter 6.

4   H G Widdowson *Teaching Language as Communication* (OUP 1978) Chapter 6.

Section 5
Techniques and Resources for Language Teaching

5.1 Collective Speaking

The language teacher must talk, for only if the pupils hear the language sufficiently, and see and hear the patterns of it presented in a certain way, are they able to imitate it successfully and to make some of it their own, using these parts creatively. 'Listen carefully because I'm going to say this only once' would, in foreign-language teaching, be a foolish policy: for the teacher's contrived repetition, supplemented if possible from other sources, is meat and drink, whatever its defects and limitations, and the class must have lots of it. This is not, of course, to deny that the teacher, even in language-lessons, can talk too much. It is essential to leave plenty of time for the pupils to talk too. How can this be done?

Let us return to our average class of children. If, in a twenty-minute period of oral work, the teacher is to speak for no more than five minutes in all – that is, for a quarter of the time, which is not excessive in the early years of learning – fifteen minutes will remain for speech by the pupils. If there are thirty of these, they will thus be able to speak for half a minute each; in other words, for $19\frac{1}{2}$ minutes they will be silent. Even if the early lessons are wholly oral, as they should be in some circumstances, the pupils will not get much more speaking-practice. In a whole week it will amount to five or six minutes at most. Nobody, however apt at language-learning he or she may be, is likely to master the basic patterns of a language very quickly with such a provision. (This is not, however, to suggest that listening is not also a valuable, indeed an essential, means of practice.)

Fortunately there is a fairly straightforward solution to the problem. If the pupils are always to speak alone, they will have few chances of speaking, and the larger the class the more silent they will have to be. Classes of over fifty or sixty are common in certain countries and in such a class, if individual speaking only is relied on, a considerable number of children will have no chance of opening their mouths from beginning to end of the lesson-period.

The solution is, of course, collective speaking. I would go so far as to say that, except in the advanced stages of a foreign-language course, collective speaking is not merely a desirable technique but an essential one. Group-work – that is, practice in small groups of about four to six pupils – is desirable too; but group-work may be concerned with reading and writing as well as with oral practice.

Like other language-teaching techniques, collective speaking has its disadvantages. One of the obvious ones is that it is more difficult, even for the experienced teacher, to detect errors of pronunciation when pupils are speaking in chorus. Further, the lazy pupil at the back of the class may at times be doing little more than moving his lips in approximate unison with his more energetic fellows, though an alert teacher will soon notice this. In collective speaking, moreover, some classes, particularly of younger children, tend to drawl or to adopt an unnatural sing-song manner in collective speaking, while others tend to shout, thus disturbing other classes.

Measures can be taken to counteract such disadvantages, but before considering these let us look at the advantages. There are several. Firstly, the genuinely shy pupil need not be exposed to embarrassment. As soon as possible in the earliest language-lessons there should, of course, be some individual speaking, but, at least to begin with and whenever a new usage is being initially practised, it is helpful for the shy pupil to take cover under the general performance while he is still struggling with his own: for language-lessons will quickly become distasteful if they make him appear ridiculous. Secondly, collective speaking, especially when alternated with individual speaking, helps to keep the oral work brisk and lively. Nobody feels left out in the cold; everybody is 'brought in' and got to participate. Thirdly, the class is given a feeling of collective effort. Fourthly, it is easier to keep the full attention of the class and to hold the pupils together in their oral language-learning activity. Lastly, and above all, collective speaking increases very greatly the amount of practice each pupil gets.

It is this last advantage which is most decisive. Collective speaking by the pupils ensures that both teacher and pupils can speak a lot, and that is one of the essentials in all-round language-learning, and perhaps even when the long-term aim is mainly to cultivate reading skill. There is no reason why every child should not speak over and over again during the lesson-period, if collective-speaking techniques are adopted. In this way all the pupils will soon get thoroughly familiar with the language-material the teacher is presenting and will begin to make it their own. If they are silent during a large part of the oral work (again, this does not rule out planned listening exercises, additionally), adequate command of the material is likely to be considerably slower in developing.

W R Lee

Speaking Together (in English Language Teaching XXIV.1 1969)

pp 31–32

1 *'Fortunately there is a fairly straightforward solution to the problem'* (lines 26–27).
   a What is the problem referred to?
   b What solution does the author offer?
   c What advantages and disadvantages are mentioned by the author? Can you think of others?

2 The author says that measures can be taken to counteract the disadvantages. What steps would *you* take to see that collective speaking is as effective as possible?

3 In your opinion, are the advantages mentioned by the author sufficient to justify the use of some practice through collective speaking? What alternative procedures could be used?

FOR FURTHER REFERENCE

1 M Finocchiaro   *English as a Second Language* (Regents 1974) pp 60–61.
2 W Rivers   *Teaching Foreign-Language Skills* (University of Chicago Press 1968) pp 42–43.

5.2 Practice in Pairs

The teacher of English is often faced with the conflicting problems of teaching large classes and the need to give them massive practice in the structures of the language. What is more, few coursebooks, if any, give sufficient practice material to ensure controlled oral drill to
5 the point of saturation in the patterns that have been taught. Understandably, many teachers take the line of least resistance to these difficulties, and limit their oral work to a minimum of class repetition and a few scattered questions.

Yet massive oral practice is possible with large numbers of
10 learners and one device open to the teacher in such a situation is to set the students working orally in pairs.

After all, the essence of language is communication; at its simplest, meaningful verbal intercourse between two people. Common patterns are found in seeking information (by question and answer),
15 seeking confirmation (by affirmation and agreement), eliciting disagreement (by affirmation and negation), or eliciting verbal action (by command and obeying). And these are some of the modes that the teacher can readily harness to paired language practice. This, at the reinforcement stage of language learning, gives a
20 communication situation in its simplest form, yet with an optimum control over the resulting dialogue.

Perhaps an example will best illustrate the advantages and potential of oral practice in pairs. Imagine the situation where the teacher has introduced defining relative clauses – with *who* and
25 *whose* (e.g. *The man who brings the milk*; *The man whose car is outside*; etc.). The learners have met and understood examples and seen how they work in context. Now is the time for practising them and the 'line-of-least-resistance' teacher sets a written exercise from the book. But this can hardly be called massive practice, and the ten
30 or fifteen sentences each student writes (even if correct) can hardly be sufficient to drive home the new patterns to the point where they are integrated with the general body of his language mastery. The written exercise certainly has its place as a slightly different kind of reinforcement, but it should be preceded by oral drill.
35 The paired practice is introduced by the teacher putting on the blackboard:

> *a nurse*
> *a librarian*

and asking: *'Where does a nurse work?'* ('A nurse works in a hospital.') Then comes the new pattern in the questions: *"Which one is the person who works in a hospital?'* ('A nurse.') and *'Which one is the person who works in a library?'* ('A librarian.')

Now the teacher adds to the blackboard list familiar nouns which fit the pattern: a waiter, a secretary, a cashier, a shop assistant, a bus driver, a teacher, an actor, a hairdresser. Then he asks the class, *'Which one is the person who works in a . . .?'* He asks five or six questions, if necessary writing up the place of work opposite each noun:

a nurse	*a hospital*
a librarian	*a library*
a waiter	*a restaurant (a café)*
a secretary	*an office*
a cashier	*a bank*
a shop assistant	*a shop*
a bus driver	*a bus*
a teacher	*a school (a college)*
an actor	*a theatre*
a hairdresser	*a hairdresser's*

Now the class is able to do its first bit of work in pairs. 'Practise in pairs,' the teacher says, 'the person on the left asks the questions; the person on the right answers.' Notice that there is no problem for the learners as to what to ask and what to answer. Notice also that the teacher has made things easy for the weaker and less enterprising students who will ask the questions they have heard the teacher ask; but the more enterprising will want to start with the questions the teacher deliberately left out.

Watching and listening carefully, the teacher decides when to change the questioners and, when he judges that the material has nearly been used up, instructs the persons on the right to ask the questions and those on the left to answer.

After a suitable time for this practice, the teacher stops the activity and prepares the class for the development of the activity. So far, all the questions have started: *'Which is the person who works in a . . .?'* But we can make the question more general by adding more nouns to the blackboard and giving more choice in the question, though still practising the same pattern.

So a new blackboard list is begun alongside the first, starting with:

a postman
a pilot

80 As before, the teacher puts the first questions to the class: *'Which one is the person who brings our letters?' 'Which one is the person who flies planes?'* Now this second list is developed on the blackboard by the addition of familiar nouns, and these are used to frame questions. Again, if necessary, a brief help towards the answer may be added.

85 a postman	brings letters
a pilot	flies planes
a farmer	grows food
an author	writes books
a musician	makes music
90 a window cleaner	cleans windows
a dentist	looks after teeth
a florist	sells flowers
a tennis player	plays tennis
an architect	designs houses (buildings)

95 After five or six questions to the class, they are told for the second time 'Practise in pairs,' with one member of each pair being the questioner to start with, and later the other. This practice continues for a suitable period – up to two minutes – before the teacher brings it to a stop and introduces a related pattern. As a reminder, he puts
100 part of the familiar pattern on the board – *'The person who works in a hospital.'* Now he asks: *'What's a librarian?'*, eliciting the answer 'A person who works in a library' and *'What's a postman?'* ('A person who brings letters.'). Two or three other examples show the class the new, related pattern of question and answer. (*'What's a . . .?'* 'A
105 person who . . .').

And the learners are ready for the third short session of work in pairs.

This particular set of twenty nouns has been selected to be used with other related patterns, using *whose*. So, after the third paired
110 practice, the teacher reminds the class of one of the *whose* patterns. *'Which one is the person whose work is in a hospital?'* (A nurse.) *'Which one is the person whose work is bringing letters?'* (A postman.) A fourth paired practice follows, and the fifth, using the same lists and a *whose* answer, is started by sample questions and answers like:
115 *'What's a waiter?'* ('A man whose work is in a restaurant.') *'What's a farmer?'* ('A man whose work is growing food.').

G Broughton
Practice in Pairs (in M Finocchiaro: *Teaching English as a Second Language* Regents Publishing Co. Inc. 1974) pp 152–155

1 a Analyse the various stages in the paired practice activity described by the author.

   b Do you agree that, for the kind of teaching situation the author has in mind, the activity is purposeful, meaningful and interesting?

2 The author mentions some common patterns of verbal interaction (lines 13–17). Suggest how the activity he describes could be adapted to:

   a seeking confirmation;

   b eliciting agreement and disagreement.

3 a Do you think that *both* collective speaking (described in the previous extract) and paired practice have a place in the classroom? If you prefer one of these procedures, give your reasons.

   b Would you use paired practice even with small classes? Give your reasons.

4 Suggest other uses for 'practice in pairs' in the classroom.

FOR FURTHER REFERENCE

1 D Byrne *Teaching Oral English* (Longman 1976) Chapter 7.

5.3 Group Work

At the presentation and practice stages of learning it is normally both economical and effective to teach the whole class as a single unit. But the 'class' is after all a purely arbitrary unit whose size may vary, and to increase the amount of practice the students can get, as
5 well as making it more realistic by getting them to talk to one another, we have already suggested dividing the class up into pairs. Our concern now at the production stage is to provide the students with an environment within which they can communicate easily and freely, and within which they can work together independently and
10 meaningfully with only the minimum amount of direction from the teacher. The solution lies in forming smaller units or groups.

We should note that the group, made up of perhaps six to eight students under the direction of a group leader (one of the students themselves), whose function is to co-ordinate the activities of the
15 group and to serve as required as a link with the teacher, is a largely autonomous practice unit. The activities which the students are asked to undertake in their groups are defined by the teacher and discussed first with the class as a whole, but once this has been done, the students should be allowed to work to a large extent on their
20 own. Divided into groups, the students are now able to sit together, facing one another in a small and intimate circle (rather like a club meeting) and talk freely. The teacher is still present and he has an important – and usually demanding – role to play in helping and advising the students as required, but he has abdicated his previous
25 one and become something like a guide or consultant.

Of course it cannot be pretended that all will go smoothly from the start. Like all procedures – from chorus work, when the students have to speak in unison, to paired practice, when they have to begin to work on their own – group activities take some time to get
30 accustomed to. (This is true both for the students and the teacher.) But the students quickly appreciate the value of self-directed activity, of being allowed to be 'agents in their own learning'. Above all, they are motivated to go on learning because they are made aware that they can use for themselves, on however limited a scale,
35 the language they are learning. It should not be forgotten that for many learners (especially children and adolescents) group activities

offer the only opportunity of putting the language to a real and immediate use.

Organising group work

(a) Structuring the group. The size of the groups has to be worked out in relation to the number of the students in the class, but as a general rule there should be between five and eight students in each group and not more than five or six groups in the class. The groups should be formed by the teacher and should include students of mixed abilities, on the principle that they will help one another in various ways. Later on the students may be allowed to change groups. Each group should have an identifying label (e.g. a name or number) and a set position in the classroom to work in so that, when the students are asked to do group work, they can begin with the minimum of fuss and delay. Usually group work will involve some re-arrangement of the classroom furniture.

(b) Group leader. Each group should have its own 'leader' (or co-ordinator – whichever label is preferred). Initially, he may have to be appointed by the teacher but, since he must be changed from time to time, the students may later be allowed to choose their own. The function of the group leader is not to dominate the group but to co-ordinate their activities and to serve as a link with the teacher.

(c) The role of the teacher. The teacher's main task is to prepare the students (sometimes by briefing the group leaders) for the activities they must undertake. Having done this, he should to a large extent leave them to get on with their work. However, this does not mean that he can sit back and relax. The students should be encouraged to consult him as the need arises and, depending on the type of activity and on the level of the students, he should visit the groups and listen in. If he participates in an activity, he should try to do so as if he were a member of the group. His job is no longer to control or correct them. But he should observe their difficulties and mistakes, noting both individual and general problems. In the light of this he will be able to shape both his class teaching and group activities in future lessons.

(d) Duration and frequency. Many factors are involved here (the number of lessons per week, the level of the class etc.) but once the students have enough language for communication activities – on however limited a scale – some group work should be carried out about once a week for perhaps half a class period. Longer sessions may sometimes be needed (to complete a project, for example, in which the students are especially involved) and in general it is inadvisable to interrupt an activity which is going well.

(e) Problems. Some teachers feel dissatisfied because group work is time-consuming, and because they cannot see their students making obvious and measurable progress. It is true that progress cannot be measured in the same way as it could at the practice stage, but it should be remembered that the students are not merely consolidating what they have learnt but also using, perhaps for the first time, what they have learnt only superficially at earlier stages. This is of great motivational value and offsets the apparent disadvantage that group work is time-consuming. It is also sometimes argued that lazy students will take advantage of group work to be even lazier! However since students usually get more deeply involved in group activities than in regular class work, laziness is certainly not likely to increase.

Students may also sometimes resort to the use of the mother tongue. This cannot always be avoided and should be accepted on occasions if it is needed to further the activity in hand. But most activities will not normally require the use of the mother tongue and adequate preparation with the class before group work begins will help to smooth out language difficulties.

Finally, there may, from time to time, be problems of 'discipline'. We have noted that it takes time for the students – and the teacher – to get used to new procedures. But the real problem is not 'active' indiscipline or bad behaviour, which can be easily detected and corrected (and in any case tends to disappear when students are involved in learning) but 'passive' indiscipline in the form of non-participation, when the students opt out of learning. This, however, is much less likely to result from group-work than from more conventional class teaching.

D Byrne
Teaching Oral English (Longman 1976) pp 80–82

1 *'The group . . . is a largely autonomous practice unit'* (lines 12–16). Explain how group work is organised and show in particular how this affects the role of the teacher.

2 *'Like all procedures . . . group activities take some time to get accustomed to'* (lines 27–30).

    a What are some of the difficulties involved in organising group work?

    b In your opinion, do the advantages outweigh the disadvantages? Give your reasons.

3   The author says that 'the group . . . should include students of mixed abilities.'

Do you agree with this recommendation? In what circumstances might you wish to form groups which were made up of students of equal ability?

4   a   Suggest various types of activity which are suitable for group work.

   b   Examine any coursebook to see what provision is made for group activities. If no specific provision is made, which activities could be adapted for this purpose?

FOR FURTHER REFERENCE

1   M Long   *Group Work in the Teaching and Learning of English as a Foreign Language* (English Language Teaching Journal XXXI.4 1977).

2   P Mugglestone in H Moorwood (Ed)   *Selections from MET* (Longman 1978) *Group Activities: Some suggestions.*

3   C Livingstone   *Streamed Group Work* (Modern English Teacher 5.1 1977).

4   D Barnes and F Todd   *Communication and Learning in Small Groups* (Routledge and Kegan Paul 1977).

5.4 Repetition within Context

Repetition and contextualisation are two of the most important activities in learning a language. In practice, however, these two activities are often contradictory. If there is a lot of repetition there is little context, and if there is a lot of context there is little repetition.
5 To supply the necessary repetition, pattern drills and substitution tables have usually been used, whereas separate dialogues and anecdotes supply contextualisation.

Most dialogues try to exemplify the teaching point, but rarely succeed in driving it home. They are generally stretches of 8 to 12
10 utterances in which the teaching point appears once or twice. A pattern drill is sometimes appended to the dialogue, where the teaching point is drilled in individual sentences, often completely unrelated to the preceding dialogue.

The problem is how to combine both the advantages of context
15 and the necessity of repetition to achieve optimum results. How can we construct drills containing repetition within context?

One solution to the problem is a type of dialogue parts of which may be expanded at will to increase the amount of natural repetition in a natural situation. We could call this a 'stretch' dialogue, since
20 the repetition within the context may be stretched to any desirable length. We shall here try to show how such a stretch dialogue works in practice, how it should be presented and used.

All stretch dialogues start from a certain core, which may be available in the textbook but in most cases will have to be specially
25 written by the teacher. The first thing to do, therefore, is to select or write the appropriate core dialogue which sufficiently illustrates the teaching point. After having presented this core dialogue, the teacher expands it at an appropriate place in order to give more repetition to the teaching point.
30 Let us illustrate this by an example. Suppose that a class at an intermediate level is about to practise the modal auxiliaries *should* and *shouldn't*.

After the presentation of the teaching point and the preliminary checking for comprehension, the teacher introduces a simple
35 dialogue by first giving an outline of the context in which the dialogue is situated. For instance: 'Mr Adams, a nervous business-

man, is just back from a visit to the doctor's, and his wife would like to know what the doctor said.'

Mrs A: Well, what did the doctor say?
Mr A: In the first place I should eat less fat.
Mrs A: I see.
Mr A: I should also take some exercise.
Mrs A: What about smoking?
Mr A: He said I shouldn't smoke so much; in fact, I shouldn't smoke at all.
Mrs A: Didn't I always tell you you should stop smoking. You didn't have to pay a doctor for that.

After the core dialogue has been mastered, it should be expanded at a place where it is possible to get maximum repetition of the teaching point. The nature of the repetition depends on the core dialogue which has been chosen. The best ones will include naturally repetitive situations, such as a customs officer greeting travellers again and again with the same series of questions: 'Where do you live? Did you buy anything abroad?' etc., or a waiter asking guests what they want to eat, etc. There are many situations where repetition is a natural part of the context and these can be exploited in the stretching process.

Keeping our core dialogue as an example, we pick a place where the teaching point can be repeated naturally within context. Mr Adams could, for instance, enumerate more of the doctor's advice on what he should do and what he shouldn't do.

Mr A: He also said I shouldn't drink so much coffee.
Mrs A: What about whisky?
Mr A: I shouldn't have any alcohol at all.
Mrs A: And what should you have?
Mr A: Plenty of rest.
Mrs A: In other words, no work.
Mr A: Precisely. He also said I should stop worrying and enjoy life.
Mrs A: Well, so should I! I think I'll go and see that doctor myself.

The teacher should now write this expanded part of the dialogue on the blackboard and proceed in the same way as he did for the presentation of the core dialogue.

It is only after both parts of the dialogue have been mastered, that the learner will be ready to take an active part in the stretching process by (1) varying the form of the teaching point, and (2) varying

151

its context.

Keeping the context of the core dialogue stable, the teacher now guides the learners into variations of its form. He can, for instance, have the learners convert the indirect speech of the dialogue into direct speech by having one learner (let's call him Peter) assume the role of Mr Adams, and the others take their turns acting the role of the doctor. 'Now, Peter is very tired and nervous', the teacher tells the learners, 'and you will advise him not to work so hard, to get more sleep, not to stay up late or anything else you think he should do.'

We might get something like this:

A: You look rather tired today, Peter. Maybe you shouldn't work so hard.

B: I think you should get a good night's sleep.

Peter: Do you mean to say that I should skip my morning classes?

B: No, I mean that you shouldn't stay up so late at night.

C: Maybe you should see a doctor.

D: I think it's football that tires you, Peter. You should do your homework rather than play so much football.

Peter: I think you should all stop criticising me.

So far the first and second person have been used in direct speech. It is now necessary to drill the teaching point with the third person. One of the learners is therefore told to ask each learner what he suggests Peter should do to overcome his fatigue. It might turn out something like this:

A: Tom, what do you think Peter should do?

B: I think he should work less and not worry about his marks.

C: Do you agree, Mark?

D: No, I don't. I think Peter shouldn't work at all, etc.

Now that the teaching point has been driven home, it should be integrated into the speech habits of the learner. This can be achieved through varying the context, thus giving the learner an opportunity to use the new form in as many situations as possible.

Keeping in mind the learners' ages, their level in the language, their social background, and their fields of interest, the teacher should now prepare the class to use the new form not only accurately and fluently, but independently.

He may proceed step-by-step in the following order:

Step 1. List a number of everyday situations such as: taking the bus, on the way to the office, at the restaurant, giving a party, etc.

Step 2. List a number of questions as to what you should do and what you shouldn't do in a particular situation. Suppose the situation he chose is 'Mrs Robinson is giving a party'. Here are a few questions he would list:

1. Do you think Mrs R should invite a lot of people or just a few friends?
2. Should she send out written invitations or should she make the invitations by phone?
3. What do you think she should serve her guests?
4. Should she serve a cold buffet or just sandwiches?
5. What drinks should she serve?

Step 3. Construct the framework for the dialogue: Mrs Robinson is giving a party. She is about to discuss the guest list and the menu with her husband, who makes a few suggestions as to what she should do and what she shouldn't do. He tells her that she shouldn't invite a crowd, but just a few friends, that she shouldn't go to the trouble of sending out written invitations, but phone the guests instead, that instead of a cold buffet she should just serve sandwiches, that she shouldn't bother about making a cake, but rather buy one at the baker's shop, and as for drinks, that she should have a variety, etc.

Once the learners are equipped with this framework, they construct their own dialogues at home and bring them to class. The teacher then chooses the best ones and has them dramatised by the learners.

These dialogues can then be written by the class in the form of short anecdotes as homework.

After the learners have mastered the technique of writing these dialogues, they may be asked to choose their own situations.

Since these dialogues are in a way 'made to measure', one cannot expect to find many appropriate ones in the traditional textbooks. The teacher can use the composition of these dialogues as an opportunity to adapt his teaching material to the specific needs and interests of his class; this is one of the best ways to gain the learner's attention and participation, to have him feel the need to express himself and thus engage unconsciously in the process of language learning.

I Schmidt-Mackey
Repetition Within Context (in English Language Journal XXI.3 1967) pp 235–240 abridged

1 a Explain briefly in your own words the concept of the 'stretch' dialogue proposed by the author and outline the various stages involved in it.
  b To what extent do the procedures suggested seem to fulfil the need to provide for two levels of language behaviour as discussed in 4.6?
  c Can you suggest alternative ways of providing 'repetition within context'?

2 Do you agree with the importance the author attaches to repetition in language learning? Give your reasons.

3 Devise a similar stretch dialogue for use at a less advanced level.

FOR FURTHER REFERENCE

1 A Hayes *Teaching Dialogues in the Classroom* (Modern English Teacher 5.3 1977).
2 G McCready *Developing a Lesson round a Dialogue* (English Teaching Forum Special Issue: The Art of TESOL Part 1 1975).
3 J Dobson *Dialogues: Why, When and How to Teach them* (English Teaching Forum Special Issue: The Art of TESOL Part 1 1975).

5.5 Language Games

Language games can add fun and variety to conversation sessions if the participants are fond of games. Games are especially refreshing after demanding conversational activities such as debates or speeches. Here, the change of pace from the serious to the lighthearted is particularly welcome, although language games can fit into any directed conversation programme quite well.

Some teachers feel that language games are more appropriate in the manipulative phase than in the communicative phase of language learning. Most teachers, however, find language games valuable in both phases. In the manipulative phase, a game is a wonderful way to break the routine of classroom drill by providing relaxation while remaining within the framework of language learning. In the communicative phase, a game can be stimulating and entertaining, and when the participants have stopped playing the game you can use it as a stimulus for additional conversation. For instance, if the group has just finished the game in which players indicate whether a statement is true or false by running to chairs labelled 'True' and 'False', you may then ask questions about what happened during the game. ('Who was the first player?' 'Who knocked the chair over by accident?' 'What was the first true statement in the game?' 'How many points did Team 2 score?' etc).

Of course, for maximum benefit from a language game in either phase, the teacher should select only the best from the hundreds of language games available. Most people would agree that a good language game (1) requires little or no advance preparation, (2) is easy to play and yet provides the student with an intellectual challenge, (3) is short enough to occupy a convenient space in the conversation programme, (4) entertains the students but does not cause the group to get out of control, and (5) requires no time-consuming correction of written responses afterward.

The following suggestions are designed to ensure the greatest success with any of the games you select:

1 Make thorough preparations for the game. Read the rules to yourself several times so that you have a good understanding of how it is played. Gather materials for the games that require

special equipment. Plan how you will direct conversation during or following the game.

2   Before introducing a game to a class, ask the students if they think they would enjoy this kind of activity. Occasionally an adult class expresses in no uncertain terms its lack of interest in the prospect of playing a game. When this happens, it is best to abandon the idea – at least for the time being.

3   Choose a game that allows as many students as possible to participate. If the class is large, a number of students will sit as the audience during some games. But even there, members of the audience may keep score and in other ways take part in the game. In small classes, you should make sure that every student has an active role in every game.

4   Be sure that the game you select is within the range of your students' ability. Remember that the students will be greatly challenged by the fact that they are playing the game in a language other than their own.

5   Do not play a game at the beginning of the conversation period. Save the game for use in the middle or toward the end of the session, when the students would welcome a change of pace.

6   Give the directions to the game very clearly, making sure that everyone understands exactly how to play. You may want to play a few 'trial' games first, just to make sure that everyone knows his role.

7   Direct the game yourself. Always stand in front of the class, so that all students can see you while you act as the leader or referee.

8   Be sure to follow the rules of the game exactly. If you do not 'stick to the rules' but permit even one student to break a rule, you will establish a precedent that may lead to hostility among the students. It is always best, therefore, to anticipate problems of this kind and to play strictly according to the rules.

9   Keep the game well under control. Even though you want your students to have a good time, you cannot allow class discipline to disintegrate. Establish a pleasant but firm tone, and the students will be able to enjoy the game and learn in the process.

10   Observe how the individual players react to the game. Students who make an error in a game may feel a bit sensitive, so you should soften any blows to pride. If you constantly encourage

a good spirit of fun, you will reduce the chances of unhappiness during the game.

11   In team games, try to have in each team an equal number of more proficient students and less proficient students. This will balance the teams and prevent embarrassment on the part of the weaker students. It also makes the contest more exciting. Some methodologists recommend that you set up permanent teams so that you do not have to name new teams each time. This has its merits, but you may prefer, as I do, to create new teams each time you play a game, thus lending variety and interest to every fresh contest.

12   If a game does not seem to be going well, try a different game. Since some games appeal to one group of students but not to another, you should be flexible in your use of games.

13   Always stop playing a game before the students are ready to quit. In other words, never play a game so long that it begins to bore the participants. Similarly, do not play one game too often, since this will cause it to lose its novelty.

J Dobson
Effective Techniques for Conversation Practice (Newbury House 1974) pp 107–109

1   a   Say briefly what you think the main function of language games is.
     b   Do you agree that they are effective at both the manipulative and communicative phases of language learning?

2   a   Which of the suggestions (see lines 33–92) do you agree with and which do you disagree with? Give your reasons.
     b   In particular, say whether you agree with the recommendation that the teacher should always direct the game himself.

3   Find some examples of games which satisfy the criteria in lines 25–30.

4   Describe any game which you have found particularly successful in promoting language learning.

FOR FURTHER REFERENCE

1   H Moorwood (Ed) *Selections from MET* (Longman 1978) *Games, Puzzles and Problems.*

2   S Holden (Ed)   *Visual Aids for Classroom Interaction* (Modern English Publications 1978).
3   W R Lee   *Language Teaching Games and Contests* (OUP 1979).
4   D Byrne and S Rixon (Eds)   *Communication Games* (NFER Publishing Company 1979).
5   A Wright, D Betteridge and M Buckby   *Games for Language Learning* (CUP 1979).

5.6 Question Practice through Games

Anyone who has ever set foot inside a classroom will realise at once that the fatuous invitation 'Now class, you ask me some questions' will not get us one step ahead in fostering this fundamental skill, for it is hardly likely to stimulate the dreamer doodling idly in the back row, or for that matter anyone else, except perhaps the infuriatingly bright learner who wishes to shine. Our duty is clearly to provide practice for all our pupils; language learning should be one of the most democratic of activities.

The teacher can employ a number of devices to evoke a variety of questions systematically from the learner in the form of situational or non-situational drill work, assisted by verbal cues or by flashcards. What we are concerned with here, however, is the less mechanical, less systematic, but more lively practice offered by games and related activities suitable for a wide range of language learners.

Unfortunately one often comes across teachers who, while they readily concede the value of games with classes of young learners, summarily dismiss them for adults. Certainly there are times when not even children feel like playing games, and it is as well for the teacher to be aware of this. If his intuition lets him down, he can ask quite bluntly 'Would you like to play a game?' and proceed according to the response. Some games are of course more suitable for children, others for adults, but this does not always depend on the players or the activity so much as on the teacher himself. If he feels he is undertaking something beneath his dignity, then this attitude soon rubs off on the learners; but his own enthusiasm for a particular game will be equally infectious.

It is worth bearing in mind, too, that a game which may seem puerile to the native speaker need not appear so to the foreign learner, who is occupied with the language involved. Adults will accept the most trivial of games if they are made aware of the rationale behind playing them – assuming there is one. The more mature student is often so eager to tackle light activities that one wonders whether in every grown-up there does not lurk an irrepressible little boy who must be appeased from time to time. It is the adolescent who proves the most contrary, for here we come up against the forces of critical young adulthood.

Let the well-meaning teacher be warned, however, that all age-groups will soon become sated and somewhat cynical if plied with
40 long-winded and pointless games thrown in when the teacher has run out of other lesson material. Games are best made purposeful by being planned into the lesson beforehand and, like a varied but controlled diet for the weak stomach, are to be given little and often. No game should be dragged on to the inevitable point of boredom,
45 no matter how entertaining it may at first seem.

As many players as possible should be involved in the playing of the games and other activities. To achieve this, large classes may have to be divided into groups under different leaders or chorus responses may be necessary, but quick-fire contributions from
50 learners named at random by the teacher will guarantee the most lively and profitable sessions.

All game-like activities benefit from the additional motivation provided by forming each class into two or more balanced teams for friendly rivalry, especially if some scoring system is instituted.
55 Scoring with younger children may be undertaken by an accumulation of items, e.g. beans, or through pictorial representation on a chart for general display. If scores for different games are accumulated over a period of a week or more to find an overall winning team, then it would be wise policy to devise some means of
60 rewarding the team members concerned, no matter how modestly. Even games with adults might be dealt with in this way – a teacher who can vouch for this is the one who generated a very keen sense of competition by presenting winners with small cut-outs glued on card depicting bottles of a popular brand of drink!
65 Not all games are an instant classroom success, for many proceed very erratically when they are introduced, despite the teacher's best efforts to ensure continuity. Familiarity with the rules and forms of the activity offers the only solution to this problem. Experience shows that this is not given most effectively by prefacing each game
70 with a detailed verbal description of procedure, but by actually embarking on the game with a minimum of preamble, leaving the rules to be explained as you move along. The sure way of learning a game is to play it.

One final point: inevitably there will be a player who cannot
75 resist the opportunity to ask a facetious or plainly absurd question when his turn comes round and class attention is focussed on him. He can be dealt with quite simply by commenting on the interesting

nature of his inquiry, then obliging him to suggest an appropriate answer.

A L W Rees
Games and Question Practice (in English Language Teaching Journal XXIX.2 1975) pp 136–137

1 Some teachers maintain that language games are only suitable for young learners.

   a What is the author's view? What reasons does he give in support of it?

   b What is your own point of view?

2 a What advice does the author give for conducting games which either complements or contradicts the suggestions listed in 5.5?

   b Say whether you agree that it is best to embark on a game 'with the minimum of preamble'.

3 The author gives the following example of 'question practice through games':

   A volunteer is supplied with an opening statement, such as 'I'm leaving town next week' and invites the class to fire a battery of questions at him. The important words in his answer must always begin with a letter designated at the beginning of the game. For example, if the letter 'S' is chosen, then the activity would be carried on something like this: 'Where are you going to?' 'To Spain.' 'When are you going?' 'Next Saturday.' 'At what time?' 'Seven in the morning.' 'Who are you going with?' 'My sister.' 'What's her name?' 'Sue.'

   Give other examples of your own.

FOR FURTHER REFERENCE

1 A L W Rees *Getting Questions Asked* (English Language Teaching Journal XXX.4 1976).

2 K Morrow *Asking Questions* (English Language Teaching Journal XXXIII.2 1979).

3 A F Deyes *Games for Advanced Students* (English Language Teaching XXVII.2 1975).

5.7 Drama and Language Learning

Drama, from the most mundane of two-sentence dialogues to the most complex literary art, focuses on language use and the concomitant linguistic and extralinguistic behaviour. Thus the use of drama serves two goals of a language programme: (a) leading the
5 students to use the language to communicate, and (b) giving them insight into the culture of the native speakers of the language. Furthermore, it approaches these goals through an activity that is rewarding and enjoyable to all concerned.

First, the student, through the use of drama, not only gains an
10 understanding of grammatical structure in context but also experiences the dynamic use of the language to influence, control, entertain, and inform.

Second, the reading and the production of plays develop for the student relevant subcultural activities through which his acquisition
15 of the new language goes hand in hand with an increasing familiarity with the culture of the language.

The product of study (the new language) and the medium for using it (the context of the drama) fuse into a language-learning process that carries with it high interest, relevance and enjoyment.

20 **Language skills**

Perhaps few would quarrel with the teaching of drama for its humanistic values, but the use of drama for teaching language skills requires more specific explication. Drama is a literary form that structures human behaviour and speech into art. Possibly originat-
25 ing as ritualised group actions or dance expressing joys and sorrows, thus depicting the history of a people, drama incorporates the generalised behaviour and language of a people. Reflecting behaviour through individual characters for the most part, it also makes use of particular differences in behaviour and speech.

30 The humble origins of dramatic action, later exalted to formalised and ritualised behaviour, can best exemplify both the utility and the appeal of drama in the language classroom. In modern times, it encompasses everything from the sublime poetic dramas of our greatest literary artists to the most ordinary, everyday conversations
35 and tribulations. Drama is clearly language in action.

In connection with teaching English, I suggest four drama activities that range from making use of minimal language skills to utilising native-speaker proficiency. In some cases these activities can add interest to the classroom. In others, they might be more appropriate for a language club or as an extracurricular activity.

Role-playing dialogues

The dialogues often used in language classrooms are miniature dramas. Although they may not be art, they contain the essential elements of dramatic incidents: characters, plot, action, resolution. They are greatly condensed, sometimes to highlight a grammatical point, sometimes to exemplify a communication context. The usefulness of the dialogues, however, can be extended by suggesting different behaviour to accompany the words. This will often necessitate linguistic changes in the dialogue as well, but the result will be close enough to the original to make the speaking task fairly easy.

The essential ingredient with respect to dramatising dialogues is action. There is very little reason for students to read dialogues from their texts while sitting at their desks. A simple dialogue such as the following is more relevant if the relationship between the speakers is indicated by appropriate physical behaviour.

> A: Hello. May I help you?
> B: Yes, I want to buy a can of beans.
> A: Green beans?
> B: No, red beans.

Alternative possibilities of language and action in the same social situation can be demonstrated and practised, making the practice of dialogues relevant to the learners.

Improvised conversations

The acting out of simple dialogues leads naturally to more complex communication situations. The language employed in these situations, however, is not necessarily more complex. Therefore teachers who prefer more contextualised language practices might start their drama activity with improvised conversations based on selected contexts.

In essence, the teacher can start an activity of this sort by identifying natural situations that require communication between two or more persons. Then he defines and describes the roles of the speakers. Then the student speakers, using the items of the new language they have previously mastered and attempting to for-

75 mulate new language utterances, engage, actually and actively, in
the tasks of communication.

One example should demonstrate this type of creative dramatic
activity. Let's assume there are two speakers, a student and his
instructor. The student has lost his term paper and tries to convince
80 the instructor that he needs more time to rewrite it. The instructor
thinks he just did not finish the assignment.

Unlike the typical textbook dialogue, this situation is likely to call
on the speakers to use a variety of tenses; affirmative, negative, and
question forms; short answers; and perhaps gestures and other
85 physical actions to convey meaning. The situation is meaningful to
the speakers, and therefore 'controlled', because they have experienced similar situations.

Play-reading groups

90 Obviously, small play-reading groups maximise practice in reading
conversation-like language. They help students become better
prepared to face real-life language situations that use the full range
of regional, social, and emotional speech.

The groups should select their own reading materials, since one of
95 the obvious benefits of such an activity is the high motivational
factor. Selections may be as academic or as much 'fun' as the group
chooses, ranging from literary classics to contemporary humorous
skits, children's plays, or controversial socio-political materials.

Play production

100 The effort required to produce a play warrants careful selection. Not
only should the play provide a context in which communication can
occur; its language should merit the hours of scrutiny and memorisation required. Additionally, as a work of art it should provide the
performers, and hopefully the audience, with an aesthetic experience
105 equal to the work required for the production. The criteria for
selecting a play for production by a language class or club are
somewhat different from those for selecting one for a drama club.
The language teacher must focus his attention partially on the
language experience provided by the production of the play.

110 The success of any amateur dramatic production can best be
judged by what the performers learn by doing the play. Some of
these learning experiences are abstract and immeasurable; only the
individual performer can judge whether he has gained anything
significant. These abstract experiences include such important
115 things as an appreciation of a literary form called drama, an
understanding and appreciation of human character through trying

to become a fictional character in a drama, an extension of one's knowledge of the variety but universality of human experience.

M Imhoof
Drama and Language Learning (in English Teaching Forum XI.4)
pp 24–25

1 The author stresses the value of drama for language teaching.
   a According to him, what purpose does it serve?
   b Why does he maintain that it is especially valuable? Do you agree with his point of view? Give your reasons.

2 a What activities does the author include under the heading of drama?
   b In your opinion, are all the activities 'dramatic'? Do you think they are all equally valuable for language teaching? Say why.

3 a What is meant by 'improvised conversations'?
   b Suggest other similar situations which could be used for this type of activity.

4 a How does play-reading differ from the two activities previously mentioned?
   b What are some of the advantages and disadvantages of this activity?
   c How would you organise play-reading for classroom purposes?

5 *'The success of any amateur dramatic production can best be judged by what the performers learn by doing the play'* (lines 110–111).

   In your opinion, what can students of a foreign language learn from this activity? Is the effort involved in producing a play likely to be justified by what the students learn?

FOR FURTHER REFERENCE

1 R Via *English through Drama* (English Teaching Forum Special Issue: The Art of TESOL Part 1 1975).
2 A Maley and A Duff *Drama Techniques in Language Learning* (CUP 1978).
3 S Holden *Drama in Language Teaching* (Longman 1981).
4 R Seely *In Context* (OUP 1976).

5.8   Songs in Language Learning

Most children enjoy singing, and songs are often a welcome change from the routine of classroom activity in learning a language. Pleasure for its own sake is an important part of language learning, a fact which is often overlooked by the teacher in his quest for
5 teaching points, or by the course designer focussing on presentation or repetition. Songs make the experience of learning English a child-centred and enjoyable one. Yet the accessibility of songs should not encourage us to be indiscriminate in our use of them, for they may help or hinder the learner in a number of different ways. They help
10 when they reinforce the teaching. In this way they can be a useful aid in the learning of vocabulary, pronunciation, structures, and sentence patterns. They hinder when they interfere with learning, when they establish irregular sentence or stress patterns which have to be corrected when used in conversation. These facts should be
15 kept in mind when considering the role of songs in language learning.

Learning takes place not merely through good presentation, but through meaningful, spaced repetition of the learning items. Since many coursebooks do not provide sufficient meaningful repetition
20 of the teaching points, the careful teacher is constantly looking for occasions to use words and sentences from previous lessons, before they fade from the learner's memory. But repetition by itself does not greatly improve learning. Rote repetition induces boredom. The teacher's task is to see that repetition is meaningful, and songs
25 provide a means of increasing the amount of repetition possible without losing the learner's interest. Songs can thus help the teacher by consolidating his teaching. They may be used to help establish (1) sounds; (2) rhythm and stress; (3) formulae; (4) syntactical items; (5) vocabulary.
30 Children enjoy trying to produce new sounds, and learning new sounds takes practice. Yet the minimal-pair drills sometimes provided for such practice rarely interest children. A carefully chosen song on the other hand, allows the child to practise a new sound or sound position without producing boredom. A song like
35 *Bounce the Ball*, for example, gives an opportunity to practise the diphthongs/ou/and/au/, and the final /l/.

Bounce the ball, bounce the ball,
Bounce the ball high,
Bounce the ball, bounce the ball,
Let the ball fall.

Blow the whistle, blow the whistle,
Blow, blow, blow,
Blow it hard, blow it loud,
Blow, blow, blow.

Learners whose mother tongue has a syllable-timed rhythm, not a stress-timed rhythm as in English, will tend to stress English syllables more or less equally, acquiring one of the characteristics of a foreign accent. The natural rhythm of songs, with a regular recurring beat between which are a varying number of unstressed syllables, happens to be the stress pattern of spoken English. Songs can thus help establish a feeling for the rhythm and stressing spoken English. *Girls and Boys Come Out and Play* gives a useful lesson in English rhythm and stressing.

Girls and boys come out and play,
The sun above is bright today,
Leave your work and leave your sleep,
Come and join us in the street,
Come with a shout and come with a call,
Come with a smile and bring your ball,
Down the steps and up the path,
All the fun will make you laugh.

Some songs contain everyday expressions which are useful in conversation. A song such as *How Are You Today?* gives practice in the pronunciation and stressing of a frequent and useful phrase.

How are you, yes how are you, how are you today?
I have come to visit you from many miles away,
I have got a gift for you,
I have got a song for you,
How are you, yes how are you, how are you today?

Sometimes a structure or sentence pattern can be fixed in the mind of the learner through a song. The following song can be used to give repetition to such patterns as *This is a pencil, Point to the pencil, Is this a pencil? Yes it's a pencil*, and so on.

This is a pencil, this is a book,
This is a pencil, this is a book,
This is a pencil, this is a book,
This is a pencil, this is a book.

Every song is an opportunity for vocabulary review, provided that it
uses the vocabulary of the school course. Some songs offer a
80 pleasant way of giving repetition to words of a particular centre of
interest or situation. *Head, Shoulders, Knees and Toes* is useful for
reviewing the names of parts of the body, and is accompanied by
actions.

Head, shoulders, knees and toes, knees and toes,
85   Head, shoulders, knees and toes,
Knees and toes and eyes and ears and mouth and nose,
Head, shoulders, knees and toes, knees and toes.

J C Richards
Songs in Language Learning (in TESOL Quarterly III.2) pp 161–163

1 Show how songs 'may help or hinder the learner'. Refer to the
   ideas discussed by the author and add any other points of your
   own.

2 What are the advantages and disadvantages of *reading verse* in
   comparison with *singing songs*?

3 In this article the author is concerned with teaching songs to
   children. Do you think songs are equally valuable for adult
   learners? Give your reasons.

4 Many coursebooks today include or are accompanied by songs
   which have been specially written for the foreign language
   learner. Do you think these are preferable to original songs?

5 Find other songs which could be used to provide practice in the
   five areas mentioned by the author (see lines 28–29).

FOR FURTHER REFERENCE

1 R Berghouse   *A Spoonful of Singing* (English Teaching Forum
   Special Issue: The Art of TESOL Part 2 1975).
2 A L W Rees *Techniques for Presenting Songs* (English
   Language Teaching Journal XXXI.3 1977).
3 A Maley   *The Use of Songs in Language Teaching* (Lingua E
   Nuova Didattica 2.4 1973).
4 J Dobson   *Effective Techniques for English Conversation Groups*
   (Newbury House 1974) Chapter 19.

5.9 Developing Reading Skills

Students need to be encouraged to read for the content of the material as they do in their own language. Meaningful reading requires concentration upon the important elements which convey the message. Constant attention to each word presents such an overwhelming amount of information that the mind cannot process it all, even in the native language. Just as in listening comprehension, the students must learn to focus their attention on message-carrying, manageable units of language in order to avoid being bogged down in a mass of detail. An analogy with boating may better describe the point being made here. As the boat leaves the dock, it must get up on top of the water in order to acquire any speed. Similarly, the students must rise to the point in reading where they are above the drag of all but the necessary information if they are to achieve any speed and enjoyment in reading.

Even after reading the entire paragraph two or three times while attempting to think in the language, the students still may not be sure of some passages, and these same sections may contain ideas which are crucial to the total comprehension of the paragraph. Therefore, they often cannot avoid a more careful examination of some difficult phrases, but they should not resort to the dictionary until all other possibilities have been found wanting. The secret is to get them to exhaust all their own devices before 'turning' for help. Often they fail to realise that the typical dependence upon the dictionary not only prevents them from really learning to read but also slows their reading. They need to be convinced that any kind of speed at all is impossible while they are dictionary dependent 'cripples'. At the same time, they should be encouraged to read using the shortcuts which they commonly practise in their own language.

One shortcut which they can carry over from their native language is the practice of guessing the meaning of words. Reading in their own language, they have acquired the almost unconscious habit of making a logical inference as to the meaning of words based on the context. Twaddell gives the following example to illustrate this point: 'The clouds parted momentarily, and the snow on the mountain-top coruscated in the rays of the rising sun.' All English-speaking students who understand the remainder of the sentence

would automatically classify 'coruscated' as being a synonym for 'sparkled', 'shone', 'glistened', etc, and proceed with their reading without even considering the use of a dictionary. The students
40 should be encouraged to carry this shortcut into second-language study, and the teacher should make it a point each day to include a few examples from the assigned reading of vocabulary words easily understood by means of sensible guessing. Any efforts on his part to improve the students' confidence in their ability to guess meanings
45 pay huge dividends in improved reading skills.

As well as applying their knowledge of the world around them to infer contextual meanings of words, the students' knowledge of language structure can also be exploited to simplify their task in reading comprehension. Some parts of speech are necessarily more
50 important in grasping total meaning than others. Since students know their own language, they should have little difficulty in deciding which are the most important elements in any given sentence from Carroll's Jabberwocky, 'Twas brillig and the slithy toves did gyre and gimble in the wabe.' to illustrate students'
55 grammatical awareness. Even if they do not know the meanings, the students still should recognise that 'brillig', 'toves', and 'wabe' are nouns, that 'gyre' and 'gimble' are verbs, and that 'slithy' is an adjective. Knowing the function of the word in the sentence helps the students to guess meanings. Even if this knowledge does not
60 provide them with any illuminating clues, they still have an advantage in that they know which words to look up in the dictionary. The fact that they can concentrate on nouns and verbs makes the task more realistic and decreases the amount of time spent in consulting the dictionary. In short, it is important that they realise
65 that a dictionary definition is not necessary for each word in the reading, and that normally nouns and verbs are the key words in the process of unlocking the meaning of difficult passages.

It is appropriate here to point out that students may not be aware of this ability to guess the meaning of incomprehensible sections of
70 assigned reading based on their knowledge of native-language grammar and the world around them. Therefore, it is up to the teacher to assist them in fully developing these abilities in the second language. He should first of all give them examples similar to those given here during the introduction to reading for comprehension.
75 Later, he should not forget to give examples of these skills in each of the reading lessons. For some time, he might point out a few before the students read the lesson and afterwards ask them for additional

examples. Thus, he can teach them to be aware of and to practise this shortcut.

K Chastain

The Development of Modern Language Skills (Rand McNally 1973)
pp 184–186

1 Students *'should not resort to the dictionary until all other possibilities have been found wanting'* (lines 20–21).

Why does the author advise against using a dictionary in the circumstances he describes? Do you agree with his point of view?

2 a What 'shortcuts' commonly used in mother-tongue reading does the author discuss? Do you agree that they are important for developing reading comprehension skills in foreign-language teaching?

b Can you suggest other shortcuts which students should be trained to use?

c What other aspects of language structure could be exploited as an aid to reading comprehension?

3 Choose a text which could be used at an elementary level to introduce students to the procedures discussed in this passage. Indicate the items which you would use in class.

FOR FURTHER REFERENCE

1 P Riley *Improving Reading Comprehension* (English Teaching Forum Special Issue: The Art of TESOL Part 2 1975).

2 V Horn *Advanced Reading: Teaching Logical Relationships* (English Teaching Forum Special Issue: The Art of TESOL Part 2 1975).

3 M J Paine *The Variation of Classroom Reading Techniques* (English Language Teaching XXVII.3 and XXVIII.1 1973).

4 J Dakin in H Fraser and W R O'Donnell (Eds) *Applied Linguistics and the Teaching of English* (Longman 1969) *The Teaching of Reading*.

5.10   Basic Principles in Teaching Writing

One principle in teaching written English seems to be that we must view the teaching of written English in two lights. First, it is a language problem – that is, a problem of assembling words to form grammatical sentences. Second, it is a rhetorical problem – a
5 problem of teaching students to organise words and patterns so as to fulfil a given rhetorical aim. (Rhetorical is an old word but by no means an out-dated one. We may here substitute for it the ambiguous word stylistic.) For example, we may ask a student to write a letter. He must, first, produce language that is 'English' as
10 opposed to 'non-English'. Second, he must organise his letter to express clearly what he wishes to say. Note that rhetoric is not the same as content. Rhetoric implies the organisation of both form and content to meet a particular rhetorical aim, such as persuading a friend to take a certain course of action, or complaining to a
15 neighbour about something, or explaining how to operate a machine or bake a cake.

With native speakers, a writing course can perhaps lay greater stress on rhetorical problems, though it must necessarily include producing the proper language. With foreign learners of English,
20 language problems should definitely play a major role, especially at the earlier stages. Indeed, R J Owens believes that the language problems of foreign students of written English are 'grossly underestimated' and that we shift the emphasis to rhetorical problems much too soon. He thinks that 'drills, repetition with
25 variations, and contextualised practice in abundance are vital to satisfactory achievement'.

Another basic principle in the teaching of written English that has emerged is the principle of controlled, or guided, writing. Controlled writing is based on a number of assumptions. One is that, as much as
30 possible, we should teach one thing at a time. Writing any type of composition involves a number of complicated rhetorical and linguistic operations, and we should break these down and teach them separately. Another assumption is that we are not teaching literary skills and rewarding only the creatively imaginative stud-
35 ents. Therefore, we should present our students with tasks that both teacher and students may assess according to more realistic criteria

172

and that the majority of the students can successfully complete. The feeling is that – especially at the earlier stages – we should not allow the students to commit more than a very few errors. That is, we should work out procedures whereby the students will be motivated by success.

The difficulty about free composition (besides its being complex in terms of what it demands from the students and thus conducive to a great number of errors) is that it is difficult and time-consuming to mark. Moreover, the marking is seldom objective but tends rather to be subjectively impressionistic. It is easier for the teacher to opt for an obvious writing talent or an imaginative interpretation of the topic than to give credit for linguistic performance in a dull composition.

On the other hand, passages of controlled composition tend to be short, with the aims of the writing task simply and clearly stated. At each point at which the student may be in error, he is either clearly right or clearly wrong according to the precise instructions of the text. That is, the student has either made a right or a wrong choice from a set of alternatives or he has transformed an active into a passive or converted a present to a past tense or substituted he for she and made all the relevant adjustments to the text – or he has not done so. Marking is therefore quick and easy for the teacher.

M Sharwood Smith
Teaching Written English (in English Teaching Forum XII.3 1974)
p 9

1 Outline briefly the two principles discussed by the author.

2 a What is meant by the term 'rhetoric'?
  b Give other examples of 'rhetorical aims'.

3 One assumption of controlled writing is that 'we should teach one thing at a time'.
  a What are the reasons for adopting this approach to the teaching of writing? Do you agree with them?
  b How important is it to ensure that students do not make mistakes when they are given writing tasks?

4 Examine any coursebook for the beginning stage of language learning to see whether it incorporates both the principles discussed in this passage.

FOR FURTHER REFERENCE

1 M Sharwood Smith *New Directions in Teaching Written English* (English Teaching Forum 14.2 1976).
2 A Raimes *Composition: Controlled by the Teacher, Free for the Student* (English Teaching Forum 16.1 1978).
3 C B Paulston *Teaching Writing in the ESOL Classroom* (TESOL Quarterly 6.1 1972).
4 W Slager *Classroom Techniques for Controlling Composition* (English Teaching Forum Special Issue: The Art of TESOL Part 2 1975).
5 D Byrne *Teaching Writing Skills* (Longman 1979) Chapter 3.

5.11   Correcting Errors in Written Composition

Whether we can control composition work rigidly or 'guide' it or give advanced students opportunities for free composition writing, mistakes are bound to occur. Our problem is to decide what to do with them. There appear to be five distinct techniques of dealing with errors:

(a) the teacher gives sufficient clues to enable self-correction to be made;
(b) the teacher corrects the script;
(c) the teacher deals with errors through marginal comments and footnotes;
(d) the teacher explains orally to individual students;
(e) the teacher uses the error as an illustration for a class explanation.

It seems to me that all these techniques have their place and that the teacher, after considering the nature of the error concerned, its frequency, and the standard of the class as well as that of the student who made it, must decide which technique is likely to be most effective.

All experienced teachers would I think agree that self-correction is the most effective way of extinguishing error, but unless the clues which can be given are quite unambiguous and are interpreted correctly, further and worse confusion is likely to result. Many teachers have evolved a number of symbols with which they indicate on the script or in the margin what the nature of the error is (e.g. Sp = spelling; t = tense error; D = wrong, missing or superfluous determiner; C = a countable noun used as an uncountable or vice versa; Sg Pl = singular and plural concord wrong).

This is an excellent system for errors which can be clearly defined and where the student has reached a high enough standard of English to be able to look at the symbol and think 'Yes, of course, how stupid of me'. For example, a student of intermediate level writes: 'Although he was there, I did not saw him for a long time.' Here I would underline saw and put Vb in the margin. (I prefer Vb = 'wrong verb form' to the more commonly used T = 'tense error' because, as this example shows, frequently students do not mistake

175

the tense they should use, but the form of the verb or its auxiliary.)

However, this technique of correction cannot deal with most lexical errors, particularly where wrong collocations are concerned. For example, a student writes 'It was a large opportunity for him'. With a very advanced student one might be able to indicate that large did not collocate with opportunity and that he must try to find a more appropriate modifier, but with most students a direct correction by the teacher on the script is preferable. And I would use this method too for a whole host of minor or careless errors where, even if self-correction were possible, one would not wish to insist on it for fear of invoking the law of diminishing returns. Self-correction ought to be reserved for those major errors which we want to remain memorable. (The correction, not the error, of course.)

There are other errors where a crossing out and correction on the script will mean very little and a symbol in the margin even less; where what is really needed is a brief explanatory comment.

This is particularly so when a structure is unacceptable within its context but would be perfectly acceptable in a different one. For example, 'He would not tell me', when the context makes it clear that inability to tell rather than reluctance was involved, or 'The watch was very expensive for me', when it was not bought because it was 'too expensive'.

Such comments are probably more effective if the teacher can find a spare moment to talk to students individually about their work. Giving back written work with brief comments while the rest of the group is otherwise occupied is the ideal way of doing this. Quite often a 'Look at this sentence again; that doesn't sound right, does it?' will elicit a correction on the spot.

On other occasions the teacher may decide that a particular error is sufficiently common for the whole class to be told about it and given a quick drill exercise to consolidate the explanation. Recently, for example, I came across 'When we opened the box, we saw that one of the glass was broken'. My first reaction was to assume that this error was due only to carelessness, until I remembered having seen quite a number of similar constructions recently and concluded that the singular subject misleads students in ignoring the need for the plural in the post-modifying phrase. This was obviously an instance where a class explanation was called for. After brief emphasis of the concept 'one out of many', the class went on to do a quick substitution drill using not only *one of* but also *the best of* and *the first of*, since these constructions lead to the same error.

It would appear then that there is no single standard method of dealing with composition errors, but that the teacher must make a

176

choice between the most appropriate and effective of several techniques.

R J Wingfield
Five Ways of Dealing with Errors in Written Composition (in English Language Teaching Journal XXIX.4 1975) pp 311–313

1   a   The author lists five techniques for correcting errors in written work. Explain briefly what each of these involves.
    b   Can you suggest any other techniques?

2   a   Compile your own list of symbols which could be used to indicate to students what kind of mistakes they have made.
    b   Do you agree that 'self-correction is the most effective way of extinguishing error'? Give your reasons.

3   Some teachers prefer not to correct all the errors in a piece of written work. What is your own view?

4   From your reading of this passage would you agree that all of these techniques have their place? Give your reasons.

FOR FURTHER REFERENCE

1   C Brumfit   *Correcting Written Work* (Modern English Teacher 5.3 1977).
2   D Knapp in H B Allen and R N Campbell (Eds)   *Teaching English as a Second Language* (McGraw Hill 1972) *A Focussed Efficient Method to Relate Composition to Teaching Aims.*
3   D Byrne   *Teaching Writing Skills* (Longman 1979) Chapter 3 and Appendix 3.

5.12   Dictation

From the purely educational standpoint, doubts about the value of dictation probably have two main causes:

   (a) Some teachers think that it is a teaching device, which it is not.
   (b) Many teachers do not know the techniques involved in giving
5   dictation, and consequently do not get the full benefit from it
       in their classes.

If dictation does not teach anything, what does it do? First of all, it gives practice in oral comprehension. Any form of listening, whether in conversation with someone else, or listening to a lecturer or to a
10 speaker on the radio, demands that we should understand what is said to us. Our attention is concentrated on sounds, without either the interference or the assistance of writing. If we do not understand what is said to us, we are wasting our time and perhaps that of the person speaking to us.
15   When we do write down what we have heard, we make the transfer from spoken to written language, and in this way prove that we have understood exactly what has been said. The written record proves our ability to reproduce spoken language in correct visual form, so that it can if necessary be passed on to others who were
20 unable to hear the original speech but want to know what was said. Most people know the old joke about the army commander in the front line who sent an urgent message to his base by a system of runners who passed the message on to each other orally. The original message said 'general going to advance. Send reinforce-
25 ments.' The message received at the base was 'General going to a dance. Send 3s.4d.' If the general had sent his message in writing he would have stood a better chance of getting the troops he needed.
   Writing down from dictation involves the student in something more than correct spelling. If he cannot spell correctly, his copy will
30 reveal his deficiencies, and it is up to his teacher and himself to correct them. But, more important, dictation obliges students to contextualise and discriminate. If I write from dictation 'I read the letter and underlined the important parts of it with a red biro' I use my knowledge of English to distinguish between the two uses
35 of/red/. If I am unaware of the need for different spellings, I may not

178

do this correctly; but if I am aware of it, the context of the words obliges me to use the appropriate spelling in each case.

Dictation, then, is not a teaching exercise but a testing exercise, and contextualisation of this kind is an excellent way of assessing a student's grasp of current speech.

As for the way of getting full benefit from a dictation session, the routine followed in public examinations in Britain is one which teachers would do well to adopt. The session needs careful planning and plenty of time. Half an hour is not too long. Nothing has brought dictation into more disfavour with inspectors and other classroom observers than the tendency of some teachers to look at their watches, having prematurely run out of material for a lesson, and say 'Ten minutes left. I think we'll have a dictation.' This leads to a hasty choice of a dictation passage and to a hurried and possibly unfinished exercise.

The routine is simple and effective. The passage itself should be chosen in advance, and the reading of it should be timed and noted. For classroom as distinct from examination needs, the content, for all but the most advanced classes, should be based on structural and lexical material already studied. If the teacher does not want to dictate as it stands a passage from a book which the class has studied, then it is his duty to compose one which will give the students a fair chance of reproducing a reasonably correct copy, at the same time including the points on which he particularly wishes to assess the effectiveness of his teaching and their assimilation.

He should read the passage three times. The first time, the students should listen in order to get a general idea of its content, without writing anything. He should then read it to be written down, having first divided it up into convenient groups of four or five words. However slowly the groups are read, he should be careful to read them as connected groups, not as separate words. He should preserve the stresses demanded by the meaning, he should not deform the pronunciations of *a* and *the*, and he should take particular care to use the weak forms of words like *can*, *to*, *at*, *of* etc., when the context calls for them.

Unlike office dictation, classroom dictation is not a speed test. Like Napoleon with his soldiers, the teacher should proceed at the pace of the slowest. He should make sure that all the students have written one phrase before he dictates the next. This is one reason why plenty of time should be allowed for the exercises.

When the writing is completed, the class should be allowed a few minutes in which to look at what they have written and make any corrections which may occur to them. After this, the passage should

be read out once more, at the same speed as for the first reading.
80 During the third reading, however, the teacher would do well to
pause at the end of every sentence or two, so that students who may
need to make a correction in a sentence just read may have time to
make it without being distracted by the need to listen to the next
sentence at the same time.

85 This is the normal examination routine. In public examinations
the examiner is instructed to read each group of words once only
when they are being written down. In class, teachers will obviously
use their commonsense and repeat any phrase that may seem to
puzzle the class. The object of classwork is to secure the best results
90 possible and it is pointless to risk leaving any student at a loss by
adhering rigidly to examination as distinct from classroom
conditions.

In an examination, the copies are collected after the third reading.
For classroom purposes another reading is advisable, except for
95 very advanced students. For this reading a correct copy of the text
should be available for each student. If the passage was not taken
from one of their books to which they can refer, the teacher should
provide duplicated copies, unless he is able to write it up in advance
on a blackboard of the easel type which can be turned round to show
100 the writing when it is needed. A fixed blackboard is useless for this
purpose. It would be too much to expect the students not to look at
the correct version while they are writing their own if it has been
written up previously. Writing it on the board after it has been
dictated wastes time.

105 During the fourth and last reading, students should look at the
correct versions and at their own copies as they listen. In this way
they are able to compare what was said with what they thought they
heard and to compare what they wrote with what they should have
written. One hopes that there is very little divergence; but where
110 there is, it is important that they should realise where, how, and why
they went wrong. This must be done immediately. If this reading is
left until another lesson the memory of the passage will have faded
and the impression left by the fourth reading will be weakened.

H Cartledge
In Defence of Dictation (in English Language Teaching XXII.3
1968) pp 227–228

'Dictation is not a teaching exercise but a testing exercise' (line 42).

a   What reasons are given for this? Do you agree with them?
b   Although the distinction made here between teaching and testing is an important one, could it be argued that dictation is also a teaching exercise?

2   The author makes a number of recommendations about the way to give a dictation. Restate these, using your own words as far as possible. Do you agree with them?

3   Consider any alternative activities which involve transfer from the spoken to the written medium and say whether you think they have any advantage over dictation.

4   From your own experience of teaching or learning a foreign language, say whether you think that dictation is a valuable exercise. Give your reasons.

5   Compose a short text (50–75 words) and prepare it for dictation by dividing the sentences up into sense groups and by marking the stressed syllables. Relate your text to a specific stage of any coursebook with which you are familiar.

FOR FURTHER REFERENCE

1   A F Deyes   *Learning from Dictation* (English Language Teaching XXVI.2 1972).
2   J W Oller in H B Allen and R N Campbell (Eds)   *Teaching English as a Second Language* (McGraw Hill 1972) *Dictation as a Test of ESL Proficiency*.
3   G Broughton et al.   *Teaching English as a Foreign Language* (Routledge and Kegan Paul 1978) pp 151–154.
4   P Riley   *The Dicto-Comp* (English Teaching Forum Special Issue: The Art of TESOL Part 2 1975).

5.13 Translation

Ever since we rejected the grammar-translation method we have been frightened of using any translation in the classroom, especially in the early stages of teaching English. But at last some of us are exercising a little more discrimination. We realise that you cannot
5 just make blanket statements like 'All translation is bad.'

Perhaps in practice a fairly large number of teachers in the field do translate sentences when they see that their pupils do not follow their dumbshow. And it often comes to dumbshow, because the pupils just don't 'hear' the language being taught. Gestures and situations
10 are frequently ambiguous. That's exactly why we normally use language for communication, of course. So why restrict a more correct, teacher-based assignment of meaning to the artificial situation created in the classroom? The pupils will not arrive at the correct answers. And, what is worse, they will continue with
15 incorrect guesses unless they are fairly systematically corrected.

This view still accepts the idea that language includes habit-formation. What it does not say is that habit is the whole story, or even that pattern practice accounts for everything. What it does say is that whatever habits are formed must be the right ones.
20 So Principle 1 is that the teacher's translation is to be preferred to the pupils'. Enlightenment is better than guesswork. When we look back at the grammar-translation method, we rightly object to it if it means making the pupils translate. But because our minds react so slowly to new ideas, we as teachers often go on for years with a
25 subconscious anti-translation complex, through careless association of all translation with a specific set of aims and methods which belong to an age when an elite acquired literacy and knowledge of literature in foreign languages.

But it not only depends on who translates. It also depends on the
30 level at which translation is done. Translators themselves can shed some light here. They will tell us that a good translator translates in clauses, if not in sentences. So we see that what's bad about translation is really the 'word for word' method. Now the teacher using situational methods is hereby warned not to translate single
35 words. However, if he 'gives the sense' by translating a whole sentence, the pupils will have no time or incentive to match the

individual words, but will be learning their new language on a broad conceptual basis. In any case, many of them will be meeting with entirely new concepts, which may be difficult if not impossible to express in their native tongue. To this extent there will be areas where translation would be clumsy. But I am thinking primarily of the earlier stages of learning, where day-to-day language is being learned. In these areas, translation at sentence level will in most cases be a one-to-one parallel match with English.

Principle 2 is therefore: teachers who use translation should translate at utterance level. Never use bits and pieces to assist the learners, or they will themselves tend to associate at the single-word level.

Principle 3 is that any use of translation involves a decision about when to use it. It is presumably obvious to most teachers that (a) all translation into the learner's mother tongue must be given after the new linguistic material has been presented; and (b) in many cases it will not be required.

We are not, then, advocating the indiscriminate use of translation by teachers of English. We are saying: use it when communication breaks down; even early in the course, if it appears at the right moment in relation to the perplexity of the learners. Don't ask pupils to do it overtly themselves. Finally, keep all translation at utterance level.

C V Taylor
Why Throw out Translation? (in English Language Teaching XXVII.1 1972) pp 56–57

1 a What reasons are given for using translation? Do you agree with them?
 b What other arguments are there for and against the use of translation?
 c From your own experience of teaching or learning a foreign language, state briefly your own point of view.

2 Comment briefly on the three principles proposed by the author.

3 *'You cannot just make blanket statements like "All translation is bad".'* (lines 4–5).

 a Do teachers still make statements of this kind?
 b Compare any recently published coursebook with one published 10–15 years ago and decide whether there are now compelling reasons why some translation should be used for the presentation of teaching texts.

4 Is translation still widely used as a teaching device in your country? In your opinion, is it correctly used?

FOR FURTHER REFERENCE

1 A R Bolitho Translation: *An End but not a Means* (English Language Teaching Journal XXX.3 1976).

2 I S P Nation *Translation and the Teaching of Meaning* (English Language Teaching Journal XXXII.3 1978).

3 J F Green *The Use of the Mother Tongue and the Teaching of Translation* (English Language Teaching XXIV.3 1970).

4 M A K Halliday, A McIntosh and P Strevens *The Linguistic Sciences and Language Teaching* (Longman 1964) pages 123–128 and 266–268.

5 D Wilkins *Second-language teaching and learning* (Arnold 1974) pages 79–83.

5.14 Teaching Pronunciation

In foreign language teaching, pronunciation is the one area where it is generally agreed that imitation is the essence of the learning process. Some people are better at imitation than others, but one thing is clear: in order to imitate correctly one must have heard correctly what is to be imitated. Unfortunately there is not so much the teacher can do to help his students to hear accurately. He can direct their attention to sound differences, give them plenty of opportunity to listen, but he cannot give them the ability to hear them. On occasion he can make the task easier by separating out the items to be heard. If the students cannot hear a /ts/ combination at the end of words like *cats, mats*, and persistently hear either /kaet/ or /maet/ or /kaes/ or /maes/, the teacher can contrast /t/ with /ts/ and /s/ with /ts/ separately. (Failure to make the plural correctly is often due to a pronunciation problem like this, as are some other apparently grammatical errors.)

As far as actual pronunciation is concerned, the teacher cannot rely upon explanations of tongue position or even diagrams and the use of mirrors. Apart from a few items such as lip or front of tongue positions, the sensory-motor skills involved are normally well below the level of consciousness and are not easy to deal with consciously. Some kind of intuitive mimicry is necessary. It is sometimes found, incidentally, that when the classroom pronunciation demanded by the teacher does not accord with that which the students hear around them outside the school, they can often mimic the required accent effectively in order to mock it, and their apparent inability to produce it in class is psychological rather than physical. Another source of help may be some noises used by the students when speaking their own language, i.e. onomatapoeic noises for sounds of birds, the wind, trains, etc. In a few cases these might constitute an English phoneme, as the sounds for the buzzing of the bee or for requesting silence do in English.

For successful imitation, students need to listen to themselves. Most people cannot readily monitor their own speech, and help from tape recorders can be invaluable. Hearing himself on tape in contrast with the speech model not only convinces the student that he has, or has not, achieved success, but gives him clues for further improvement.

As with all learning, motivation is a highly significant factor in pronunciation. The more it can be made necessary for the student to 40 improve his speech, the more rewarding will the teaching be. Motivation can be real or simulated. Where it is possible, actual contact with speakers outside the class in real communicative contexts (shops, etc.) is of course ideal. Where this is not possible, games in the classroom which are so designed that either hearing 45 correctly or speaking correctly are built in as an essential part of the game provide a context where communication is felt to depend on accurate speech. For example, a class can be divided into teams, standing or sitting in rows. The first person in each row is given an instruction to whisper to the next person, who whispers it to the 50 next, and so on down the line. When the last student has received the instruction he must obey it quickly. If it is worded to highlight a pronunciation point so that an error in speech or recognition at any point along the row might occur, students will in fact be engaged in pronunciation practice in a meaningful context. Thus, if the 55 instruction were 'Draw a ship on the blackboard', and the students had difficulty distinguishing /i:/ and /ɪ/, the row which produced the drawing of a sheep would not be the winner!

Given the aim of encouraging accurate imitation, the teacher's choice of what to teach and in what order to teach it depends partly 60 on his decision as to what sound features are essential for intelligibility in the variety of English he has to teach. The degree of difficulty which these sound features present to the students is governed largely by the sound patterns of their native language. By comparing the sets of phonemes and their commonly used allo- 65 phones in the native language and English, the teacher can assess the areas of pronunciation where difficulty is likely to occur. He will not necessarily be able to predict exactly what errors the student will make, but he will know which sounds or supra-segmental aspects will cause trouble. Although the different languages of the world have 70 all drawn on different sounds and sound features from the infinite range that the human vocal tract could produce, the underlying principle of system of distinctive contrasts with permitted variations is common to all.

Native language interference applies equally strongly to the 75 supra-segmentals. Foreign judgements of the English as unfriendly, or even as very polite, are often based on faulty interpretation of their intonation, whereas the English judgement of certain foreign speakers as rude or aggressive is usually based on a likewise faulty interpretation. The native language habits of intonation and stress

and general tone of voice are so all-pervading and deeply ingrained and further out of awareness than vowels and consonants, which can often be physically demonstrated, that people find it difficult to accept that there is a systematic variation from one language to another. Thus, if a foreign speaker makes a segmental pronunciation error, he is excused as a foreigner and his speech is interpreted more or less correctly depending on the context. But if he makes a supra-segmental error, a judgement is made of his personality, not of his language. Thus a German might call someone and use a falling intonation, 'Mr Smith!', as would be appropriate in German. This
will make him sound authoritative and possibly impolite in English, for gentle polite calling requires a rising intonation. Such intonation differences are a source of misunderstanding even among native English speakers from different regions.

G Broughton et al.
Teaching English as a Foreign Language (Routledge and Kegan Paul 1978) pp 58–61 abridged

1 For pronunciation 'imitation is the essence of the learning process'. In the light of this statement explain what steps can be taken to help students improve their pronunciation. Refer in particular to any techniques which you have found effective.

2 The authors give one example of a game which provides 'a context where communication is felt to depend on accurate speech.' Give other examples of similar activities.

3 With reference to any language with which you are familiar, mention some of the difficulties which speakers of that language would have, at both the segmental and supra-segmental level, when learning English.

4 What sort of goal in terms of pronunciation do you think it reasonable to set for most foreign learners? How much class time would you be prepared to devote to the teaching of pronunciation?

FOR FURTHER REFERENCE

1 H Moorwood (Ed) *Selections from MET* (Longman 1978) Section 3 *Pronunciation.*

2 A C Gimson in R Quirk *The Use of English* (Longman 1968) Supplement 1 *The Transmission of Language.*

3 P Strevens *New Orientations in the Teaching of English* (OUP 1978) Chapter 7.

5.15 Teaching Vocabulary

Here are ways in which we can help the learner understand the meaning of a word by using different approaches:

Demonstration – by showing an object or a cutout figure
– by gestures
5 – by performing an action
Pictures – by using photographs, blackboard drawings, illustrations cut from magazines or newspapers
Explanation – by description
– by giving synonyms or opposites
10 – by putting the word into a defining context
– by translating

We can help the learner connect the form of a word with its meaning by presenting the form and meaning together, so that the learner knows they are connected to each other – and this knowledge is 15 firmly implanted in his automatic responses.

Techniques for creating interest

Unless there is some challenge, the learner may not be interested enough in learning new vocabulary to give his full attention and enthusiasm to the task. Without interest, he will not pay attention 20 to the teaching. We can add challenge and interest to the teaching by:

1 Making it difficult for the learner to get the form of the word.
2 Making it difficult for the learner to get the meaning of the word.
25 3 Making it difficult for the learner to connect the meaning and the form.

Making it difficult, as I use the phrase here, means that the teacher does not give the 'answer' (form, meaning, or form-plus-meaning) directly to the learner. He forces the learner to guess, or to follow 30 clues by the teacher or found in his own previous knowledge. Thus he must use his reasoning and interpretative abilities to find the answer. In other words, the teacher and the learners play games. The teacher must be careful to see that he makes the job difficult enough to challenge the learners but not so difficult that they give up. Instead, he should help them towards a sense of achievement – a feeling of having won the game.

Let's consider ways to make the three aspects of learning a word (as listed below) difficult for the learners – to provide challenges that are real but are not so difficult as to discourage the learners:

1   We can add interest and challenge to the teaching (and learning) of the form of a word by:

a)   Altering the arrangement of a word – for example, by scrambling the letters or writing the word upside down or right to left. When the teacher uses scrambled letters, he can write the letters (out of order) on the blackboard and ask the learners in turn to guess the first letter by pointing to it, then the second letter, and so on. Or he can say the word and ask the learners in turn to put the letters written on the board in the right order by using the pronunciation as a guide.

b)   Making it difficult for the learner to identify the parts of a word – for example, by writing them in code, or by teaching the form tactilely without allowing the learner to look, or by saying the word without letting the learner see the teacher's mouth.

c)   Making it necessary for the learner to choose the form from among other possible choices. The most common example of this tactic is requiring the learner to find words in a passage that match the set of meanings given at the end of the passage. The teacher can make this exercise easier by putting the meanings in the same order as the words appear in the passage – or harder by mixing up the order. He can make it easier by providing a dash for each letter in the word, right by the meaning. Or easier still by giving the first letter of the word and a dash for each remaining letter. Another way is to write many words on the blackboard. Then as the teacher quickly says one of the words written on the board, a learner must point to the proper word. To be most effective, this procedure must be carried out with rapid-fire speed.

2   We can add interest and challenge to the teaching of the meaning of a word by making it difficult for the learner to identify the meaning. For example, when the teacher uses real objects, he can wrap them in tissue paper or cover them with a cloth and let the learner guess what the object is by feeling it or simply by contemplating its disguised appearance. Or the

teacher can have the learners close their eyes while he taps the
object or hits it against the desk, and the students guess what
the object is by listening to the sound it makes. If the form of
the word is also new, the teacher should repeat it many times
during the activities, with the learners indicating what they
80 think the meaning is by pointing, drawing, or translating.

When the teacher uses demonstration to teach the meaning, he can
perform a given action in such a way as to be slightly ambiguous,
and the learners guess in turn what the meaning is. Later the teacher
checks by asking the learners to translate the new word into the
85 mother tongue.

When he uses drawings, the teacher might draw a series of dots on
the blackboard and invite the learners in turn to connect the dots up
in such a way as to make a picture of what the word means. The
teacher might make this game easier by numbering the dots or by
90 telling the student who is performing at the board when he has made
a correct connection. He might refine this game by letting the
individual learner draw one line at a time – and continuing to draw
only as long as he draws each succeeding line correctly. When the
teacher uses cutout figures, the learner can be blindfolded as he tries
95 to identify the cut-outs.

When the teacher uses verbal explanations, he can employ many
of the techniques used to introduce interest when teaching the form
of the word. For example, he can write the meaning (synonyms,
opposites, synonyms in the mother tongue, a description) in code or
100 with scrambled letters. Or he can omit some of the letters of the
words in the meaning. Another useful and adaptable technique is the
game 'What Is It?' Here the teacher gives clues about the word he is
teaching, but he makes sure that the first clues are general enough to
force the learners to think hard. Here is an example. The teacher is
105 dealing with the word refrigerator, which the learners do not know
yet. He says (and note that he uses the word in each clue):

A refrigerator is useful.
A refrigerator is big.
A refrigerator is usually white.
110 A refrigerator has a door.
A refrigerator uses electricity.
It is cold in a refrigerator.
A refrigerator makes ice.

People put food in a refrigerator.

I S P Nation

Techniques for Teaching Vocabulary (in English Teaching Forum
XII.3 1974) pp 18–20

1   Under the three headings of *demonstration, pictures* and *explanation* the author refers to a number of ways in which the learners can be helped to understand the meaning of new words.
    a   Give examples of words which could be taught in these ways.
    b   Which of these techniques do you think would be especially useful in the early stages of language learning?

2   a   Why does the author stress that we need to add 'challenge and interest' to the learning of new words?
    b   Evaluate the various techniques which he suggests. Are there any which you think would be of limited value with an average class of thirty learners?

3   The author gives an example of how the word refrigerator could be taught by verbal explanation. Choose three other words and show how you would teach them in a similar way.

4   Suggest other procedures for teaching vocabulary which the author has not mentioned.

5   From your experience of teaching or learning a foreign language do you think that sufficient attention is paid to the teaching of vocabulary in the early stages? Examine any coursebook of your own choosing to see:
    a   whether there is adequate provision for the learning of vocabulary;
    b   what procedures are used.

FOR FURTHER REFERENCE

1   J C Richards in K Croft (Ed) *Readings on English as a Second Language* (Winthrop 1980) *The Role of Vocabulary Teaching.*
2   M H Laforest   *On Teaching Vocabulary* (Lingua E Nuova Didattica VIII.2 1979).
3   D Wilkins   *Linguistics in Language Teaching* (Arnold 1972) Chapter 4.
4   J Haycraft   *An Introduction to English Language Teaching* (Longman 1978) Chapter 5.

5.16 The Place of Grammar

Language teaching theory has tended to emphasise the rapid development of automatic speech habits, and the need to discourage students from thinking consciously about the underlying grammatical rules. Advocates of the 'oral method', the 'audio-lingual 5 method' and the 'multi-skill method' in their more extreme forms have assumed that language learning is an inductive rather than a deductive process, and that the most effective method of teaching is to provide plenty of oral and written practice, so that students learn to use the language spontaneously without the need for overt 10 grammatical analysis. Recently, however, a change of attitude has been apparent among writers on second language teaching methods. The experience of a large number of teachers over many years suggests that a combination of inductive and deductive methods produces the best results. It is now generally acknowledged that 15 language learning is not simply a mechanical process of habit-formation, but a process which involves the active co-operation of the learner as a rational individual. Far from being the passive recipients of stimuli in the form of exercises and drills, students learn in a selective manner, searching for the information they need to 20 discover the system of the language being learned.

Most teachers will continue to see language learning as fundamentally an inductive process based on the presentation of data, but one which can be controlled by explanations of a suitable type. An important question concerns the nature of the grammatical explana-25 tions given to the students, and the type of linguistic grammar from which these explanations should be drawn. Clearly if language teachers are to be called upon to make judgements about what constitutes an appropriate treatment of grammar for classroom use, it will be an advantage if they are conversant with the main 30 developments in modern grammatical theory. We believe that a knowledge of grammatical theory is an indispensable part of every language teacher's training, even if in many cases this knowledge will reveal itself in the teacher's general attitude and approach to problems, rather than directly in the construction of specific 35 diagrams and exercises.

What we are advocating, then, is the reinstatement of some

explicit description of the grammar as an essential element in both first and second language teaching. This does not mean that we are suggesting a return to the so-called 'grammar-translation' method of language teaching, under which students did not easily achieve a fluent use of the spoken language, because they spent much of their time studying abstract grammatical rules, memorising word-lists and translating from the native to the target language, and vice versa. We do believe, however, that in any given classroom situation just so much attention should be given to grammar as may be necessary in order to promote quick and efficient language learning. Thus we see the teaching of grammar not as end in itself, but as a useful aid in helping students to achieve the practical mastery of a language.

J P B Allen and H G Widdowson
Grammar and Language Teaching (in J P B Allen and S Pit Corder (Eds) *The Edinburgh Course in Applied Linguistics Volume 2* OUP 1975) pages 44–46

1   The authors maintain that *'the teaching of grammar is a useful aid in helping students to achieve the practical mastery of a language'* (lines 47–49).

What arguments do they use to support this point of view? Do you agree with them? Give your reasons.

2   Give examples of the kind of rules and grammatical explanations which language learners generally find useful.

3   Do you agree that a knowledge of grammatical theory is an indispensable part of every language teacher's training? Give your reasons.

FOR FURTHER REFERENCE

1   S Pit Corder   *Introducing Applied Linguistics* (Penguin Education 1973) *Pedagogic Grammars.*
2   W Rivers   *Teaching Foreign Language Skills* (University of Chicago Press 1968) Chapter 3.

5.17 Visual Aids in Language Teaching

The term 'visual aids' suggests in the first instance things brought into the classroom, like wall charts, slides and films – something extra, possibly non-essential, which *helps* the teacher to do his job better. This may be a reasonable point of view when thinking about 5 the geography lesson, but in the language classroom it is far too narrow. The language teacher cannot do his job *at all* without visual help or without resorting to translation.

Let me redefine visual aids in the language-teaching situation. *Anything which can be seen while the language is being spoken may be* 10 *a visual aid.* The wrinkles which are formed when the teacher frowns are visual aids; they give meaning to his 'I'm not satisfied with your behaviour, Johnny'. The conductor's badge Johnny pins to his lapel is a visual aid and gives meaning to his 'Move along along the car, please'. And the yawn Mary gives is a visual aid and lends meaning 15 to her 'Oh I'm so sleepy'.

Everything belonging to or brought into the classroom, animate or inanimate, is a potential visual aid – teacher, boys, girls, pets, plants, clothes, furniture, materials, objects; everything that anyone is seen to do, any movement he makes, any action he performs – 20 laughing, crying, smiling, working, acting, misbehaving, attending or not attending – all are potential visual aids; the moment any member of the class or the teacher begins to speak in English, the whole classroom and its contents are instantaneously converted into potential visual aids.

25 This is why the present limited meaning of the term 'visual aids' is perhaps unfortunate – it implies something *extra*, something imported as a frill, as a motivator but not as something central to and integral with the learning process. This does not mean that we should not talk about the part visible things can play in language 30 learning, nor does it mean that we should reject the help that the new techniques of mass communication – film and television – can give us. On the contrary. But their proper use must grow from an understanding of the relationship between the seen and the spoken.

When various traditional 'visual aids' are discussed, they tend to 35 be divided into such groups as wall charts, book illustration, 'realia' models, puppets, maps, film strip, moving film, television. These classifications are natural and often helpful, but they relate to the different *media of visual aids*, not to a significant difference of *function in the teaching process*. There is another way of classifying visual aids which may help us to understand their function better, and hence help us to use them better and more imaginatively in the classroom.

The division I suggest is between visual material (this comprehends everything I have been talking about, including the conventional visual aids) for talking *about* and visual material for talking *with*. There is, of course, no hard and fast line between these two types. The division is made principally in order to draw attention to the relation between 'things' and 'language' in the world outside the classroom, which it is meant to reflect.

To take an example: a pair of scissors can be used for talking *about* and talking *with*. The teacher may bring them into the classroom; he may talk about them, their shape and material, their uses. He can ask the pupils about them and get them to describe them. These are well-tried and familiar techniques and correspond to the use generally made of conventional visual aids. But such language behaviour is normal *only in the classroom*. Nobody, except perhaps cutlers, describes and talks *about* scissors in the world outside. In fact, although describing and talking about physical objects and pictures is a perfectly proper use of language, it is not very common in everyday social intercourse; it occurs more often in specialised academic, technical, artistic situations, and in what we might call 'demonstration situations'. This is what I call talking *about* things or using visual material for talking *about*.

Now an example of how the same object, a pair of scissors, may be a thing for talking with. The children are given scissors, combs, mirrors, or models of these things which they have made themselves (the making gives a wonderful opportunity for 'situational teaching'). They then set up a barber's shop in the classroom and act the parts of barber and customer spontaneously, or following a script they have written. Hence they are not talking *about* scissors; they are not talking *about* anything. They are simulating a situation in which language is a perfectly natural element, a situation with which they are familiar and of which a pair of scissors is as much an integral part as the language or the characters who use it.

Plenty of examples of 'things' come to mind, which can be used both for talking *about* and talking *with*: tools, instruments, money, clothes, toys, and, of course, the familiar model shop. And why, if the teaching is in a secondary school, not actually 'invade' the other teacher's territory? Go into the physics, chemistry or biology

80 laboratories, or in the gymnasium, or into the garden to help the gardener, if there is one. What you can't bring into the classroom, you may be able to take the class to see. Better the real thing to talk *with* than a picture of it to talk about.

S Pit Corder
A Theory of Visual Aids in Language Teaching (in English Language Teaching XVII.2 1964) pp 85–87 abridged

1 a Why does the author object to the term 'visual aids' in the context of language teaching?
 b How does he suggest it should be redefined? Do you agree?

2 Explain the distinction the author draws between *talking about* and *talking with* visual material and show how it is important for language teaching.

3 The author suggests that the language teacher should 'invade the other teacher's territory'. Even if you are not teaching in a secondary school, what opportunities could be provided for teaching 'through' other subjects?

4 Choose any standard 'visual aid' (e.g. flashcards, wall charts, slides etc.) and show how this can be used for *talking with*.

5 Examine any recently published coursebook to see what visual material is provided for *talking with*.

FOR FURTHER REFERENCE

1 W A Bennett *The Organisation and Function of Visual Material in Second Language Learning* (Visual Education 1970).
2 D Case *Using the Real Thing* (Modern English Teacher 5.2 1977).
3 N Hill *Notes on materials which will encourage students to talk* (Modern English Teacher 5.2 1977).
4 A Wright *Visual Materials for the Language Teacher* (Longman 1976).
5 S Pit Corder *The Visual Element in Language Teaching* (Longman 1966).
6 S Holden (Ed) *Visual Aids for Classroom Interaction* (Modern English Publications 1978).

5.18　The Nature of the Language Laboratory

The laboratory offers certain facilities which cannot be reproduced in the classroom. The facilities are most fully exemplified in a laboratory in which every student has his own tape recorder. The tape recorder is equipped with earphones which enable the student to listen to the material recorded on his own tape without disturbing the rest of the class. Through a microphone he can also record his own voice. He can play back his recording to check for mistakes or to compare his own efforts with a model version already recorded on the tape. There is a connecting channel between the teacher and the student so that the former can listen to what the student is doing and discuss any problems with him without interrupting the work of other pupils.

The effect of the machinery is to isolate each learner from his fellows in several different ways:

1　Each learner can work all the time. He no longer has to sit idly while other pupils answer questions or show the teacher what they can do. He can work uninterruptedly either at listening to material on his own tape or at trying to improve his speech.

2　Each learner can work at his own pace. He no longer needs to be either held back or out-stripped by the pace of learning of the rest of the class. He can stop the tape whenever he is in doubt, replay each section as many times as he wishes, and repeat each exercise till he is satisfied with his performance.

3　Each learner can work on his own materials. There is no longer any need for him to listen to the same materials or do all the same exercises as the rest of the class. He can be given work which matches his own needs and interests.

4　Each learner is responsible for his own performance. He is spared the embarrassment of having other pupils listening to all his mistakes. Instead he must learn to correct himself when he goes wrong, and to seek advice from the teacher when he is in doubt.

5　Each learner receives individual attention from the teacher.

It is easier to list these possibilities than to exploit them. They
35 present a formidable task to a teacher who attempts to do so. He
must have a sufficient amount of material to keep each of his pupils
uninterruptedly engaged. But he cannot expect them all to do the
same amount of work during the laboratory periods and should
adjust any follow-up in the classroom accordingly. In addition to a
40 common core of work which he may want all his pupils to do at some
time, he must provide a whole library of ancillary materials for
learners with special difficulties or interests. Since he cannot give too
much of his time to any single student, he must design the materials
so that each can learn on his own with a minimum of supervision.
45 Difficulties, misunderstandings and mistakes which could be dealt
with as they arose in the classroom must as far as possible be
anticipated or forestalled in the design of laboratory materials.
Every step must be planned and recorded in advance.

The laboratory thus frees the student at the cost of tying the
50 teacher. It makes instruction more individual, but at the same time
more impersonal. To use it effectively, it must be determined what a
student can learn better on his own with only occasional supervision
from the teacher, and what requires interaction between the student
and the teacher, or between one student and another, and is
55 therefore more suitable for the classroom. We must decide, in effect,
what can be planned in advance and performed in isolation, and
what should be improvised in face-to-face contact.

J Dakin
The Language Laboratory and Language Learning (Longman 1973)
pp 2–3

1 The author notes several advantages for the learners which are
provided by the type of language laboratory he describes in his
first paragraph.
a What are the advantages?
b Which of these advantages could be made available to the
learners, either wholly or partially, through oral work in
pairs or small groups?

2 *'The laboratory frees the student at the cost of tying the teacher'*
(lines 49–50).

Comment on the difficulties of organising effective language
laboratory work. Do you think these difficulties outweigh the
advantages noted earlier?

3 From your experience of language teaching, do you think that language laboratories are:

a essential? (What alternative facilities are there?)
b desirable? (Do most students enjoy and benefit from language laboratory work?)

FOR FURTHER REFERENCE

1 S Moulding *Meaningful Work in the Language Laboratory* (Modern English Teacher 6.1 1978).
2 W R Lee *Language Laboratories and the Learning of Foreign Languages* (English Language Teaching Journal XXX.3 1976).
3 A Howatt and J Dakin in J P B Allen and S Pit Corder (Eds) *The Edinburgh Course in Applied Linguistics Volume 3* (OUP 1974) *Language Laboratory Materials.*
4 P Strevens *New Orientations in the Teaching of English* (OUP 1977) Chapter 13.
5 *ELT Materials: Design and Use, No 2: Oral Practice in the Language Laboratory* (British Council 1978).

Epilogue   What I hope for in a classroom

Students

1 I hope to find the students involved in whatever they are doing, contributing to it and getting satisfaction from it on many levels of personality.

1 That is to say, I hope not to find them concentrating on merely coming up with correct responses (even in a structure drill), or on grinding out correct sentences or free conversations just for the sake of grinding out correct sentences or free conversation.

2 I hope to find the students comfortable and relaxed, even in the midst of intense intellectual activity or vigorous argument.

2 (a) This does not mean that they are loafing on the job. In fact, students who are really comfortable with what they are doing are less likely to loaf.
(b) This also means that the students are not apprehensive that they will be punished if they fail to live up to the teacher's expectations.

3 I hope to find that the students are listening to one another, and not just to the teacher. I also hope that they will be getting help and correction from one another, and not just from the teacher.

3 This means that the students are not like separate lamps plugged into a single power supply, in such a way that the power used by one diminishes the voltage available to the rest.

Teacher

4 The teacher is in general control of what is going on.

4 This does not mean that everything the students do comes as a direct response to a specific cue from the teacher.

5 The teacher allows/encourages/requires originality from students, whether in individual sentences, or in larger units of activity, or in choice among a range of techniques.

5 This does not mean anarchy or chaos.

6 One of the first things I notice is whether the teacher seems relaxed and matter-of-fact in voice and in manner, giving information about the appropriateness or correctness of what the students do, rather than criticising or praising them.

6 The teacher does not, either by word or by unspoken message, say to students, 'Now always remember . . .', 'You shouldn't have forgotten . . .', 'You are a good/poor student', or 'Now try to do this so that I may judge you on it'.

E Stevick
Memory, Meaning and Method (Newbury House 1976) pp 159–160

Acknowledgements

We are grateful to the following for permission to reproduce copyright material:

Edward Arnold (Publishers) Ltd. for extracts from *Second-Language Learning and Teaching* by David Wilkins, 1974; The British Broadcasting Corporation for an abridged extract from 'Adults as Learners And Classroom Management' by J Rogers from *Teaching Languages*, 1976; The British Council for an extract from pp. 19 and 20 'The Production of Functional Materials' by K Johnson and an extract from pp. 25–27 'Teaching Pupils to Acquire Language' by C J Brumfit from *ELT Documents*; the author, Maurice Imhoof, for an extract from his 'Drama and Language Learning' from *English Teaching Forum* XI.4; Longman Group Ltd. for an extract from pp. 80–82 *Teaching Oral English* (Longman Handbooks for Language Teachers Series) by Donn Byrne, 1976, an extract from *The Linguistic Sciences and Language Teaching* by Halliday, McIntosh and Strevens, 1964, an extract from *The Language Laboratory and Language Learning* (Longman Handbooks for Language Teachers Series) by J Dakin and an extract from p. 6 *Writing English Language Tests* (Longman Handbooks for Language Teachers Series) by J B Heaton; McGraw-Hill Book Company for an extract from pp. 2–4 *Testing English As A Second Language* by D Harris, copyright © McGraw-Hill Book Company. Used with permission of McGraw-Hill Book Company; Modern English Publications Ltd. for an extract from 'Integrating Reading and Writing' by Ron White from *Modern English Teacher* 6.3 1978; Oxford University Press for extracts from *The Edinburgh Course In Applied Linguistics* edited by J P B Allen and S Pit Corder, vol. 2 (1975) and vol. 3 (1974); Oxford University Press and the authors for the following extracts from *English Language Teaching Journal*: an extract abridged from 'Language and Culture' by J R Gladstone, pp. 114–117 Vol. XXIII.I; an extract from 'The Factor of Purpose in Grammar Teaching' by I Morris, pp. 38–39 Vol. XXI.I; an extract from 'New Perspectives for Language Study 2: Semiotics' by David Crystal, pp. 210–211 Vol. XXIV.3; an extract from 'The Teaching of English as Communication' by H G Widdowson, pp. 15–18 Vol. XXVII.I; an extract from 'Some Basic Assumptions Affecting Course Design' by L G Alexander, pp. 95–97 Vol. XXX.2; an extract from 'Aims and Objectives in Language Teaching' by R Roberts, pp. 224–227 Vol. XXVI. 3; an extract from 'English As She Is Heard' by K James and L Mullen, pp. 21–22 Vol. XXVIII.I; an extract from 'A Note on Writing Versus Speech' by M Sharwood Smith, pp. 17–19 Vol. XXXI.I; an extract from 'Using Connectives in Elementary Composition' by V Horne, pp. 154–155 Vol. XXVI.2; an extract from 'Speaking Together' by W R Lee, pp. 31–32 Vol. XXIV.I; an extract abridged from 'Repetition within Context' by I Schmidt-Mackey, pp. 235–340 Vol. XXI.3; an extract from 'Games and Question Practice' by A L W Rees, pp. 136–7 Vol. XXIX.2; an extract from 'Five Ways of Dealing With Errors In Written Composition' by R J Wingfield, pp. 311–313 Vol. XXIX.4; an extract from 'In Defence of Dictation' by M Cartledge pp. 227–228 Vol. XXII.3; an extract from 'Why Throw Out Translation?' by C V Taylor, pp. 56–67 Vol. XXVII.I and an extract from 'A Theory of Visual Aids in Language Teaching' by S Pit Corder, pp. 85–87 Vol. XVII.2. Reprinted by permission of Oxford University Press; Newbury House Publishers Inc. for two extracts, one abridged, from *Speaking in Many Tongues* by Wilga Rivers, 1972, an extract from *Memory, Meaning and Method* by E Stevick, 1976, and an extract from *Effective Techniques for Conversation Practice* by J Dobson, 1974; the author, I S P Nation, for an extract from his 'Techniques for Teaching Vocabulary' from *English Teaching Forum* Vol. XII.3 1974; Penguin Books Ltd. for an extract from pp. 19–21, 27–29 and 256–257 *Introducing Applied Linguistics* by S Pit Corder (Penguin Education 1973). Reprinted by permission of Penguin Books Ltd.; Rand McNally and Company for an extract from pp. 184–186 *The Development of Modern Language Skills* by K Chastain, 1973; Regents Publishing Co. Inc. for an extract from pp. 152–155 'Practice in Pairs' by G Broughton from *Teaching English as a Second Language* by M Finocchiaro, 1974; the author, Wilga Rivers, and Modern Language Journal for an extract from 'Listening Comprehension' from *Modern Language Journal* 50 (1966); Routledge and Kegan Paul Ltd. for two extracts from pp. 178–180 and pp. 58–61 (abridged) from *Teaching English as a Foreign Language* by G Broughton et al; Seido Foundation for the Advancement of Education for an extract from *From Pattern Practice of Communication* by D P Cosgrave, an article which originally appeared in Modern English Journal, 1970–71, published with the permission of Seido Foundation, Ashiya, Japan; the author, Michael Sharwood Smith, for an extract from his article 'Teaching Written English' from *English Teaching Forum* XII.3, 1974; Teachers of English to Speakers of Other Languages and the author, Jack Richards, for an extract from 'Songs in Language Learning' from *TESOL Quarterly* 3:2, copyright 1969 by Teachers of English to Speakers of Other Languages. Reprinted by permission of the publisher and author; Teachers of English to Speakers of Other Languages and the author, Dr. W R Slager, for an extract from 'Creating Contexts for Language Practice' from *TESOL Quarterly* 7:1, copyright 1973 by Teachers of English to Speakers of Other Languages. Reprinted by permission of the publisher and author; University of Chicago Press for an extract from pp. 215–217 *Teaching Foreign Language Skills* by Wilga Rivers; University of Michigan Press for an extract from 'Second Language Learning' by J C Richards from *A Survey of Applied Linguistics* edited by R Wardaugh and M D Brown, 1976.